I'm Your Biggest Fan

I'm Your Biggest Fan

KATE COYNE

NEW YORK   BOSTON

Hachette Books
Hachette Book Group
1290 Avenue of the Americas
New York, NY 10104
hachettebookgroup.com
twitter.com/hachettebooks

First edition: June 2016

Hachette Books is a division of Hachette Book Group, Inc.
The Hachette Books name and logo are trademarks of
Hachette Book Group, Inc.

The publisher is not responsible for websites
(or their content) that are not owned by the publisher.

Library of Congress Cataloging-in-Publication Data

Names: Coyne, Kate.
Title: I'm your biggest fan / Kate Coyne.
Description: First edition. | New York : Hachette Books, 2016.
Identifiers: LCCN 2016005232 | ISBN 9780316306270 (hardback) | ISBN
  9781478937425 (audio download) | ISBN 9780316390149 (ebook)
Subjects: LCSH: Coyne, Kate. | Periodical editors—United States—Biography.
  | BISAC: BIOGRAPHY & AUTOBIOGRAPHY / Personal Memoirs. |
  BIOGRAPHY & AUTOBIOGRAPHY / Editors, Journalists, Publishers.
  | BIOGRAPHY & AUTOBIOGRAPHY / Women.
Classification: LCC PN4874.C7655 A3 2016 | DDC 070.92—dc23 LC record
available at http://lccn.loc.gov/2016005232

Printed in the United States of America

RRD-C

10 9 8 7 6 5 4 3 2 1

To my men . . . and my mom.

Contents

I'm Your Biggest Fan

Robert Downey Jr. Thinks I'm Emotionally Unhinged

LET'S CUT TO THE CHASE: TOM CRUISE IS INSANELY charismatic, so much so that you do feel as though you could maybe, kind of, possibly, convert to Scientology for him. Charlize Theron is so stunningly beautiful it's hard not to reach out and touch her face just to make sure she's real and not carved out of some sort of highly rare and expensive marble that's lit from within. Kelly Ripa is hilarious and warm and bawdy and she makes you want to be her best friend or her babysitter or anything that would involve getting to call her whenever you wanted and hearing her latest outrageous story (the ones you're hearing on morning television are *beyond* sanitized). Cindy Crawford has no cellulite—believe me, I stared long enough to make sure. And yes, there are stars who are so cold and aloof and rude that you want to slap them, and others who are so incredibly kind and gracious that you want to write their parents a thank-you note for raising them right.

When I tell people what I do for a living, that I'm a celebrity magazine editor, these are the things that everyone wants to know. Yes, I've met a lot of stars, from Reese Witherspoon to George Clooney, from Jennifer Lopez to Jennifer Garner (and yet not Ben Affleck, surprisingly). When it comes to the mega-famous, I've watched them get their hair cut, change their clothes, and barely eat their meals (and I've almost always picked up the check). None of them will remember me. Which is probably for the best. Because if they did, they would likely remember someone who, at least momentarily, acted completely thunderstruck.

I come by it honestly. Before I was a magazine editor, before I was a journalist, before I was a gossip columnist or a reporter or an intern, I was a fan. And not just any kind of fan. A super-fan. Which, if we're going to be completely honest, also means I was a huge nerd.

I am an only child, and both of my parents worked full-time. After fourth grade, when I was no longer small enough to need a full-time babysitter, my "nanny" was the Zenith television that sat in the dining area of our apartment. The local syndicated channel showed reruns of *Little House on the Prairie*, followed by *Facts of Life* and *Diff'rent Strokes*. You know that scene in *Rain Man*, where Tom Cruise is throwing the playing cards down onto the hood of the car and Dustin Hoffman can recite every single one that has fallen, and which cards should still be left? I can do that. Only not with cards. I can tell you the name of nearly every actor who was on a sitcom from the mid-eighties until today. I'm not talking about Gary Coleman. I'm talking about Shavar Ross, who played Dudley on *Diff'rent Strokes*. The twins who played Carrie Ingalls? Lindsay and Sidney Greenbush. And it's not as though the TV was shut off the minute my parents arrived home; throughout the 1980s, NBC's primetime lineup blared from multiple sets in our apartment. *Gimme a Break!*, *Family Ties*, *The Cosby Show*—I knew these people as if they were my actual friends, neighbors, and siblings. I fully believed that if I lived in a house in the suburbs I'd be able to convert a space in either the attic or the garage into a full-blown apartment with skylights and a massive bathroom. I was completely prepared for an adorable cousin/suddenly orphaned tween/ street urchin moppet I'd never known existed to suddenly come to live with us. I mean, if these things could happen on *Full House*, *Gimme a Break!*, *Growing Pains*, *Happy Days*, and *Who's the Boss?*, why not in my life? Solving a problem with an elaborately choreographed lip-sync routine seemed like a fine idea: hey, it worked for the Huxtables! I could spot a Very Special Episode within the first two minutes—and knew which ones to watch with rapt attention (Alex Keaton gets hooked on speed! Alex Keaton's friend dies suddenly and he has to go to a shrink! Alex's uncle, aka Tom Hanks, comes to town and is a drunk! Basically, all the *Family Ties* VSEs were keepers) and which ones to avoid (Albert Ingalls's girlfriend gets raped by a masked psychopath; poor Dudley is molested by a creepy old man—who, of course I remember, was played by Gordon Jump, best known for his work on *WKRP in Cincinnati*).

Years later, I carried my commitment to pop culture all

the way to a new continent when, as an undergraduate at Oxford, I got my mother to ship me FedEx boxes filled with tapes of the NBC Thursday-night lineup, which at that point included *Friends*, *Seinfeld*, and *ER*, none of which were airing in the UK yet. Other students became popular at Oxford by being the best source of weed or pharmaceuticals; I was the sole hookup for the comedic antics of Matthew Perry. I still take credit for introducing George Clooney to an entire subset of young British women (that subset being "former boarding school students who generally had two first names and two last names, like Sarah Claire Boyd-Flanders and Mary Helen Barbour-Jacket). I was obsessed with most things TV-related. My love extended, albeit with somewhat less fervor, to movies and music, yet in the same semi-psychotic way: I really liked Wham! but I worshipped George Michael. I enjoyed *Dead Poets Society* but Ethan Hawke was clearly meant to be my future husband. The play wasn't the thing: the star was.

The first time I actually saw a living, breathing celebrity, I was thirteen years old. It was an Off-Broadway production of a play called *The Heidi Chronicles*. My mother owned an advertising agency that handled the majority of the shows on Broadway, which is why I was at a feminist Wendy Wasserstein dramedy, not because I was particularly evolved for my age. (Although, thanks to my mother's job, I had perhaps been the only eight-year-old to know the lyrics to every song from *A Chorus Line*. Still do, in fact.) My mom brought me to the play undoubtedly to inspire some sort of intellectual fervor in me. Or she couldn't find a babysitter. Either way, I was actually happy to be there, because I had discovered that an actress named Sarah Jessica Parker had one of the smaller roles. And though this may have been decades before *Sex and the City*, it was definitely after a little masterpiece called *Girls Just Want to Have Fun*, starring the future Carrie Bradshaw, had been released on VHS, allowing me to view it approximately 343 times.

While I may have adored SJP, her boyfriend at the time was of even greater interest. Robert Downey Jr. had starred in *Less Than Zero* just the year before. Though I was technically too young to see it in theaters, my friends and I had perfected an air of aged nonchalance unique to Manhattan-raised children, and so we sailed into the multiplex on 84th Street and Broadway without a sideways glance. Though the point of the film was ostensibly to swoon over and sympathize with poor Andrew McCarthy (and covet Jami Gertz's hair), I couldn't take my eyes off tortured, tragic Robert. Instantly, a crush was born. Six months later, standing in the lobby of the Playwrights Horizons theater in the West Village as Wendy Wasserstein wannabes (frizzy hair, glasses, all carrying a whiff of Zabar's) wiped away tears after the final act's poignant scene, I looked up and there he was. Hair artfully disheveled, eyes glassy from what I assumed was an emotional reaction to the play: Robert Downey Jr.

I gasped and grabbed my mother's arm. "Mommommom-mommommommom," I said in one long exhale. "Oh my god, that's Robert Downey Jr. *Oh my god.*"

My mom smiled. "Is he that musician you like?" she asked. I had no idea who she could possibly be confusing him with—none of the musicians I intended to marry someday had a name that sounded anything at all like Robert or Downey, and there were no Jrs. among them. No, wait. Harry Connick Jr. There was him. Still, I rolled my eyes.

"Noooooo!" I hissed. "He's the hot guy from *Weird Science* and *Less Than Zero*! Mooooom! I looove him!"

My mom patted my arm. "So why don't you go over and tell him that? Why don't you go ask for his autograph?"

I looked at her as though she'd just suggested I go over and ask him to give me my first Pap smear.

"Yeah, right," I sneered. "Are you crazy? No way! I'm not going over there! I wouldn't even know what to say!"

It's important to note here that in her job, my mother not only dealt with actors, but she dealt with Broadway actors—a very particular, and often especially high-strung and neurotic, breed. Broadway fame isn't like regular fame: it is at once more intense and more mundane. Performing live eight times a week leads a star to feel perhaps more exceptional than his celluloid and small-screen brethren. Earning next to nothing while doing so and, aside from opening night reviews, hardly ever getting recognition, can result in a bruising clash between ego and reality. Yet my mother knew just how to calm these people, soothe them into a place where they could perform in a commercial and believe that maybe, just maybe, theirs was the show that wouldn't close after only a month of performances.

"Sweetie, let me tell you something," she said. "There is not an actor alive—not a single one—who doesn't want to be told that you love his work. They all want to hear how wonderful they are. Trust me. Go tell him."

It is the second most useful piece of advice my mom ever gave me. (The first being "Never go down a flight of stairs with your hands in your pockets.") I use it to this day. (The staircase advice, too. I'm a klutz.) Even if I'm dealing with the most self-important, ego-inflated star in the universe, I find myself wanting to earnestly lean forward and say, "I hope you don't mind me saying so, but your performance in *Insert Movie Title Here* was just incredible. I thought you were fantastic." I know, on paper, how cheesy and insincere that sounds. But here's the thing: I pretty much really mean it. Your movie may be terrible, but I probably loved you in it. Or at least appreciated some aspect of what you were trying to do. And more often than not, the star—no matter how self-important or ego-inflated—responds with genuine gratitude, and even better, a slight dropping of their armor.

But at age thirteen, standing three feet away from Robert Downey Jr., I hadn't exactly perfected my game yet. I tried to play out in my mind what the worst-case scenario was. If I took my mother's advice and walked over there and politely asked for an autograph, and maybe casually mentioned that I enjoyed his performances in several films, I figured that at the very worst, he'd tell me I was bothering him and order me to walk away. In which case, I'd be humiliated...and without an autograph. As opposed to what I was at that very moment: terrified...and without an autograph. The odds seemed in my favor that at the very least, he'd be polite while saying no, which would mean I'd have virtually nothing to lose just by asking. How humiliating could it be to listen to a star simply say "No autographs, thanks"? (Incidentally, years later I learned just how humiliating, when I sat in front of Katharine Hepburn—a notorious refuser—in a theater, and a fellow patron asked for her autograph. "My dear, you know better than to ask me that," Hepburn admonished him, and the man slunk away, mildly embarrassed. All in all, it wasn't that terrible.)

I took a deep breath, spun around and, armed with my mother's advice and a felt-tip pen from her purse, marched over to Robert Downey Jr. He saw me approaching and stopped the conversation he was having to look down at me, kindly.

"Well, hello," he said before I'd even opened my mouth.

"I love you so much," I replied.

This is the point in the story where I wish I could tell you I was kidding. Or that at least I followed up with a witty, "And I'm sure you feel the same way about me." But I didn't. I just stood there. Mortified. As I realized that there absolutely was something worse than a celebrity ordering me to walk away, which was this: a celebrity being nice to me while I dissolved into a puddle of drool in front of him. I looked down at the floor and frantically wished it would swallow me whole. I looked back at my mother and thought for a moment about running straight back to her. All while Robert Downey Jr. gave me the sort of half smile that now earns him $50 million per film. Then I remembered the piece of notebook paper that my mother had given me.

"Um…I meant to say that I'm a big fan. And, um, could I have your autograph?" I said, faintly aware of my voice sounding as though I'd just sucked on some helium.

"Of course! Thanks for coming over here. It's nice to meet you. I'm Robert," he said, and held out his hand. As if I didn't know his name. As if it were genuinely nice to meet me. As if he were so honored to be shaking hands with an acne-ridden, braces-wearing adolescent who thought the epitome of cool was wearing two scrunchies in her ponytail at once. (In my defense, at that moment in time, it kind of was.)

"I...I'm Katie," I said, shaking his hand and praying my palms weren't sweaty, then offering him the ripped piece of paper.

"Well, Katie, I think it's great that you came over to say hi to me," he said. "Did you like the show?"

He may as well have asked me if I wanted to run away to Bora Bora with him. I was stunned that he wanted to know anything about me, at all.

"I did! I thought it was great! And, um, Sarah Jessica was really good, too! And, um..." I trailed off, unsure of what to shriek at him next.

"Well, I'll tell her you said that, Katie," he said, handing me back the piece of paper. "I hope you have a great night."

I took it back, fully trembling now, and suddenly desperate to flee before I made an even worse blunder. Like wetting my pants.

"Thank you so much. You have a good night, too," I said, and turned to find my mom.

I had gotten about ten steps away when I looked down at the autograph. My mom was standing next to me, smiling and asking, "See? That was easy, right?"

On the piece of paper, he had written: *To Katie. I love you, too! Robert Downey Jr.*

And with that, I burst into tears. I had thought at first that maybe I was simply going to start laughing at how quick-witted he'd been. But no, as soon as the first noise escaped my throat, it rapidly morphed into some strangled-animal sob that was fueled by gratitude for this star's kindness, admiration for his talent, and full-on awe at my proximity to him. The words banged around in my head in singular form: *Robert. Downey. Loves. You.* Remember when The Beatles performed on Ed Sullivan, and everybody in America lost their shit and those girls in the audience were shrieking and screaming? And when they'd show those girls, there was always that one other girl, standing next to the shrieking ones, who was so over-whelmed with love for John, Paul, George, and Ringo she was just quietly, desperately, bawling? Turns out, I was that kind of girl.

"Mom, we have to get out of here immediately," I said, my nose running. "Oh my god." For much of my life, people have commented on the shape of my eyes—almond-shaped or feline are the kindest descriptors I've received, while many have guessed at vague ethnicities that I don't possess. In case you don't feel like gazing at the author photo of me on the back of this book, just know that I have Renée Zellweger's old eyes. And one thing is certain about them: When I cry, my eyelids explode like a threatened puffer fish. Within min-utes, my irises become nonexistent. As my sobs continued, I could feel my eyeballs being rapidly pushed back into my skull. "Mom, let's *goooooo*," I wailed.

I turned and attempted to make a beeline toward the door, keeping my head down so no one could see my blubbering. Which meant that I didn't realize when, two seconds later, in a crowd of people streaming out of the theater, I head-butted Robert Downey Jr. right between the shoulder blades.

"Hey," he said, as he spun around and saw me, now beet-red, snot-nosed, and borderline blind. I clearly had gone through a total nervous breakdown in the four minutes since he'd last seen me. Still, he somehow recognized me.

"Are you okay?" he asked, seeming genuinely concerned.

"Me? Oh, I'm fine," I said, choking back a post-sob hiccup. "I'm just...the play really got to me. Okay, bye." I pushed past him and ran out onto West 4th Street, where my mother soon caught up to me.

By the end of our cab ride home, I had calmed down. I folded the piece of paper carefully and stored it in my purple lockbox where I kept my most prized possessions, such as the cocktail napkin from the Hard Rock Café where I'd celebrated my twelfth birthday. (Yes, I still have it.)

Within two years, I would become a girl who chased Shirley MacLaine down the street for her autograph (she declined; I survived) and followed Carly Simon into a bodega for hers (she agreed and signed the back of my math homework). I stopped fearing total humiliation, because as far as my adolescent self was concerned, I'd already survived it: I'd embarrassed myself in front of the man of my dreams and yet I had lived another day. I didn't realize it then, but that night with Robert Downey Jr. a precedent had been established, one that would follow me into my adult life. One that would actually become a career. What I learned from both Robert and my mom that evening was as simple as this: When it came to celebrities, all of them wanted to be told that you loved them and their work. And I, in ever new and creative ways, really wanted to be the one to tell them.

Chapter 1

Kathie Lee Gifford Helped Save My Soul

I HAD BEEN STARING AT MY COMPUTER SCREEN for five minutes, during which I had answered two calls and three e-mails, and I still couldn't think of it.

Ample assets?

Terrific tush?

Ravishing rear?

I noticed Richard Johnson—my boss over the past year, and the head of the *New York Post*'s legendary gossip column Page Six—hang up his phone. From the two-desk distance between us, I tried to get his attention.

"Richard!" I yelled. He was always "Richard." Never "Rich" or "Richie" and absolutely never, god forbid, "Dick." I stood up from my seat so I could see him.

"Richard!" I shouted again. "What do we call Jennifer Lopez's ass?"

"Bodacious booty!" he hollered back.

I promptly typed the phrase into the item I was writing about Jennifer's appearance at a party the night before. And somewhere, the part of my mother that had bragged to all her friends during my years at Oxford died just a little.

I wasn't supposed to be here. After graduating with a degree in English Language and Literature, a distinction that ostensibly meant I could speak knowledgeably on everything from *Beowulf* to *Bright Lights, Big City*, I assumed I would nab a low-paying but honorable job in the ink-stained trenches. Fact-checking for the *New Yorker*. Fetching coffee for a glamorous editor at *Vanity Fair* or *Vogue*. Sorting through the slush pile at a publishing house with a two-century history. From there, I would slowly work my way up, dazzling editors with my work ethic and intellect until I ultimately landed some senior-level editorial position by the ripe old age of thirty.

Then two things happened: One, none of those places wanted to hire me. Two, a friend of a friend of a colleague at a magazine where I'd been interning (for a stipend so paltry I qualified for food stamps) knew Richard Johnson, and recommended me when there was an opening at Page Six. The *New York Post*'s gossip column was a fixture of the paper so popular that it no longer even ran on the sixth page but rather had landed on page nine, so that more advertisers could buy space on the coveted pages before and after it. To say I was an inappropriate fit for a column notorious for its take-no-prisoners attitude and breakneck pace is an understatement.

When I went to interview with Richard Johnson and Steve Cuozzo, one of the paper's chief editors at the time, I wore a pink linen Laura Ashley shift dress. Not just pink linen—pink linen with large cabbage roses printed all over it. I also brought three copies of neatly stapled packets of all my best journalistic efforts at that point—paragraph-long items for the magazine where I'd been interning, focused on squabbles within the Parks Department and minor incidents involving junior staffers in the Giuliani administration. I slid my articles across Steve's desk as he tried to hide his bafflement. The girls who normally arrived to vie for this job probably boasted a long list of publicist connections, nightclub sources, and a driving ambition to be on the right side of a velvet rope. (They also had probably not set foot in Laura Ashley since they were nine years old.) I, on the other hand, had an item about the mayor banning reporters critical of him from certain events, which I had titled *Forgive Us Our Press Passes*. That clever turn of phrase right there was probably my biggest achievement to date.

Richard, when I met him, seemed as bemused by me as Steve had been. Heavy-lidded and handsome, his mouth was often fixed somewhere between a smirk and a smile. But he gamely took my packet of clippings, and later that night he must have either gotten drunk or decided a nerd in cabbage-rose print was just the jolt his column needed, because within two days I came home to a message on my answering machine that said, "It's Richard Johnson at the *Post*. Gimme a call. I have good news for you."

It absolutely was. On my first day, I walked into the *Post* newsroom, a wide space filled with row after row of desks manned by reporters shouting to each other, while a steady clatter of clicking keyboards mixed with the crackle of a police scanner. It was every scene from every one of my favorite journalism movies and shows—it was *All the President's Men* and *The Paper* and *Lou Grant* and that one season of *The Wire*—come to life. I silently thanked the *New Yorker* publisher who had rejected me and the Condé Nast Human Resources head who had never returned my calls. Because now, here, surrounded by people in jeans and T-shirts literally running down the halls after the next story, I realized I was exactly where I was supposed to be.

That feeling only grew once I met my new coworkers. As the head of the column, Richard was assisted by a team of three: that now meant me, as the most junior member, plus a rotating staff of freelancers headed up by Jared Paul Stern, who was famous, or infamous, for frequently wearing a fedora, pocket square, and three-piece suits. In his early twenties. I'm not kidding: he constantly looked like he'd just walked out of the pages of *The Great Gatsby*. The column's staff was rounded out by the senior reporter under Richard, Jeane MacIntosh. She was feisty and well sourced, someone who could coax anyone into revealing their darkest secret...and then grant her permission to print that secret for millions to read. Fair-skinned and blonde, Jeane was a single mom in her mid-thirties, fond of wearing faux-leather pants and pale, flesh-toned lipstick (it was the nineties; she was hardly alone) who could wolf down Wendy's for lunch without gaining a pound. She quickly took on a big sister role, complete with a sense of protectiveness toward me and moments of mostly good-natured tension. (Our desks were adjacent and on more than one occasion she had to endure listening to me on the phone squabbling with my boyfriend du jour or worse, just generally dissolving into a fit of whiny narcissistic navel-gazing.)

Richard, meanwhile, was my first real boss. As first bosses go, he was practically perfect, operating with equal parts parental guidance and benign neglect—admonishing me if I'd straggled in too late after a night at some premiere, but never questioning which events I was covering or why, and believing in me when I'd suggest leads that might be worth tracking down further. To be clear, I was far from an ace investigative journalist. I loved being part of a newsroom, but it was obvious to me that there was a certain type of person who was thrilled to get a call at 2 a.m. alerting them to a plane crash in Long Island that needed to be covered, and I was not that person. Luckily, at Page Six, very little chasing was necessary: people were desperate to be in the column, and just as many were desperate to call us up, confidentially, and reveal what they knew, whom they'd seen "canoodling" (a Page Six term for hooking up that has since become widely used) and which marriage was about to implode. This is one of the biggest things I learned during my time at Page Six: if you want a secret kept, tell it to absolutely no one. As Benjamin Franklin said, "Three can keep a secret if two are dead." Tell even one person, just *one*, something that you want kept quiet and here's a guarantee: it will spread. Sooner or later, anyone who knows anything about someone else is unable to resist sharing it with a third party. Once the first domino falls, it's only a matter of time before you reach someone with loose lips. At Page Six, half the job was simply picking up the phone when that last domino decided to call.

It was a thrill, of course, to see what doors the words "Page Six" would open in New York City. It was still before TMZ blanketed the world with their unique blend of paparazzi photos and gossip—and even before camera phones—so that type of pushy invasiveness was never a part of how Jeane, Richard, and I worked. As much as someone could be nice while trying to dig up dirt on you, we were. Mostly, I spent hours at parties and clubs, at premieres and the gatherings that followed, keeping my eyes and ears open for anything interesting. Sometimes a celebrity would drunkenly make out with another celebrity. That passed for headline news in our world, in which Leonardo DiCaprio was king and an impossibly obnoxious club called Moomba was his kingdom.

But it didn't mean that what we were doing—what I was doing—was harmless. The *Post* was (and remains) owned by Rupert Murdoch, an Australian billionaire well known for his staunch conservative leanings. The paper had never been bipartisan, but all attempts at objectivity flew out the window the minute the Monica Lewinsky scandal exploded. I, who had been raised on the then-bohemian Upper West Side of Manhattan by two lifelong Democrats, arrived at the *Post* just as the Starr Report was being circulated and the president was giving his deposition. Bill Clinton had been the first person I'd ever been old enough to vote for, and I had done it proudly. Now I was working at a paper that had called for his impeachment, and more importantly, on the very column that had gleefully dubbed Monica Lewinsky the "Portly Pepperpot" and did it as often as possible.

Still, at the column we were able to tell ourselves that the people we wrote about had it coming, and were doing the sorts of things—fighting, lying, cheating—that deserved to be exposed. We were simply reporting on the behavior of public figures. One of those public figures was Michael Douglas, whose messy split from his first wife, Diandra, had been covered exhaustively by the *Post* years earlier. By the time I arrived at Page Six, Michael was already dating Catherine Zeta-Jones, his life with Diandra was long in the past, and he rarely appeared in the column. But that didn't seem to matter the night I met him.

It was after the premiere for the latest post–*Basic Instinct* thriller that starred Douglas. The party following the film was held in some nondescript event space with several separate rooms, guaranteeing that even without any area specifically designated as VIP, pretty soon one room would have all the celebrities packed into it: water always finds its own level.

Sure enough, after about a half hour, I found Michael standing at the bar located all the way in the back, waiting for his drink. Taking a deep breath, I sidled over to him and offered my standard opening line at events like this one. "Congratulations on the film," I said. "I thought it was fantastic."

Michael turned to me and smiled graciously. "Why thank you," he said. "I appreciate that."

Anxious to stop him from walking off, I was ready with a follow-up. He'd played something of a bad guy in the film, a step up from his usual lecherous cads and into true villain territory.

"I hope you don't mind me saying so, but you make an excellent villain," I said. "Was it fun getting to play a bad guy again? You basically haven't done so since *Wall Street*…"

"Oh, it was a great time," Michael said pleasantly, probably offering the boilerplate answer he had prepared for questions as routine as mine. It surprised me, then, when he went a bit further.

"You know, it's interesting that you think of Gekko as a villain," he said, referencing his *Wall Street* character. "He's a little more complicated than that, wouldn't you say?"

"Yes, of course," I said quickly. As if I was in any way going to disagree with Michael Douglas at his own movie premiere. It was also dawning on me that I was having a bona fide conversation with a mega–movie star, and I was desperate to keep it going. Maybe I could draw him out on what he thought constituted a villain, and get an item out of it somehow. *Michael Douglas: I'm Not a Bad Guy!*

"And I think your character in this film was somewhat complicated, too," I offered. "I mean, you do get to see what's driving him to the brink, and I think that humanizes him beyond your typical bad-guy..."

"Yes! Exactly!" Michael said, grinning broadly at this point. I inwardly danced in place a little bit, feeling giddy that I had won his approval and that he still hadn't walked away. Suddenly, though, I realized he was asking me a question.

"What did you say your name is?" he was inquiring.

"Oh, I'm sorry. I'm Kate. Kate Coyne. From the *Post*." That last distinction was important: nothing he said to me would be useful in an item if I hadn't identified myself as a reporter. I continued smiling at Michael, but noticed that his face had shifted slightly, his eyes narrowed a little bit.

"You're not from Page Six are you?" he asked.

This couldn't possibly be leading anywhere good. Obviously, answering yes wasn't going to be what he wanted to hear. But I couldn't lie, especially as I was still hoping to quote him for the next day's column.

"Uh...yes, I am," I said, hoping my voice wasn't shaking.

Michael downed the rest of his drink and put his glass back on the bar.

"Well, Miss, let me give you a piece of advice," he said pointedly, his smile now gone. "Quit that job before your soul turns black."

Before I could respond he had turned and walked away, back to the confines of a table filled with his friends and publicist.

I was surprised at how rattled I felt, a feeling that didn't fully wear off until the next day when I recounted the story to Jeane.

"Oh my god, the same thing happened to me with him!" she exclaimed. "He said that to me at some thing at the Rainbow Room, and then left me standing there on that stupid revolving dance floor." She laughed, and I joined in. Soon it would become just another anecdote: That Time Michael Douglas Shamed Me. It was a funny story. Until it wasn't anymore.

Barely into my twenties, I was making more money than I had ever thought I would so soon after college, and yet it was scarcely enough to cover the costs of living in Manhattan. My salary afforded me the luxury of not having to live with a roommate, but on more than one occasion I found myself anxiously checking my bank account to see if my paycheck had cleared yet because I was out of cash. So when I got a call from Joanna Powell, the entertainment editor at *Good Housekeeping* magazine, with an offer for freelance work, I eagerly said yes. I had been referred to Joanna by a mutual friend, and she was looking for a reporter to help her with a write-around.

A write-around is exactly what the name implies: a means of writing *around* the celebrity in question, by talking to other people *about* the star, rather than *to* the star directly. When a magazine wants to do a story about a celebrity, but that celebrity declines to participate, the magazine has two choices: kill the story or do a write-around. Old quotes from the celebrity in question are often used; the telltale sign of a write-around is the phrase "has said," as in: "My family is my number one priority," Jennifer *has said*. That's the giveaway that the star said it elsewhere, and probably a while ago, and probably to someone else, rather than talking to a publication directly. Of course, there's a double standard at play here. No one calls a *New York Times* profile on Obama and his administration a write-around if the president hasn't granted an interview; it's simply a reported piece. But when you put Julia Roberts on the cover of a magazine without ever talking directly to Julia Roberts? That's a write-around.

Now Joanna was calling to see if I might be able to get some reporting on Kathie Lee Gifford. A few months earlier, Kathie Lee's husband, Frank Gifford, had been caught on camera by a tabloid "canoodling" with a buxom stewardess. Not long before that, a different exposé had revealed that much of Kathie Lee's clothing line for Wal-Mart was being made by child laborers in foreign sweatshops. It was not shaping up to be a good year for Kathie Lee. Not surprisingly, *Good Housekeeping*—which had featured interviews with her countless times in the past—knew they'd do well with her on the cover. Even less surprisingly, Kathie Lee had declined to do an interview at that moment in her life. So *Good Housekeeping* decided it was time for a write-around.

I was asked to get anyone within Kathie Lee and Frank's inner circle to talk about how they were holding up. As this was for *Good Housekeeping*, I didn't need to dig for dirt: the order of the day was for quotes about Kathie Lee's strength, Frank's remorse, their continued unity as a couple. Because this was pre-Google, and when Yahoo! was barely out of their Paleolithic Era, I began hunting the old-fashioned way. I pored over old stories about Kathie Lee, circling the names of friends or colleagues mentioned. Her hairdresser. Her childhood friend. Her neighbors. Then, after a string of calls to 411 in various states, I tracked down those hairdressers, friends, and neighbors. When I got them on the phone I was sure to emphasize that I was calling for *Good Housekeeping*, and that I only wanted to talk to them about Kathie Lee's grace under pressure and her continued bravery in the face of adversity. Some people hung up immediately. Others did not, and instead talked to me about Kathie Lee's grit, her ability to maintain a sense of humor in the face of humiliation—while always careful not to reveal anything too personal about the woman herself.

More searching through newspaper clippings turned up a

name I hadn't considered trying: Astrid Gifford, Frank's wife before Kathie Lee. While I had talked to plenty of people about Kathie Lee, I had very few people talking about Frank. What were the odds I could get Astrid Gifford on the phone? I called directory information in the town where she'd most recently been reported to live and asked for her listing. I was stunned when a recording promptly gave me the number.

As the phone rang, I was sure I was going to find that it was a mistake: this would be a different Astrid Gifford, one who had never heard of Frank. But the woman who answered the phone—cautious, but still upbeat and pleasant—was indeed Astrid Gifford, former wife of Frank. When I identified myself as working for *Good Housekeeping*, she only paused for a moment before starting to talk.

"I think Kathie Lee did a very smart thing in forgiving him," Astrid said, before offering her take on the situation. "I think the whole thing happened because here's a guy who was a huge star... and suddenly he's in the background holding her sheet music. That's got to hurt his pride so much. And you know what men do when they feel like that: they go out to prove something."

Slightly salacious and on the record: it was a dream speed-ball of a quote. I compiled all my reporting—including a lengthy interview with a Christian marriage counselor who had advised the Giffords—into one long document and sent it off to Joanna.

Two days later my phone rang. It was Ellen Levine, the editor in chief of *Good Housekeeping*. I would later learn, from experience, that Ellen—a silver-maned force of nature who deservedly got the nickname Queen Levine from none other than Oprah Winfrey—did not often mince words. In this case, she got right to the point.

"Is this all your original reporting?" she asked me.

"Yes," I replied, wondering what else it could possibly be.

"What I mean is, you didn't pick these quotes up from other stories, or stuff you found elsewhere? You actually got Astrid Gifford and their marriage counselor and all these other people to talk to you?" she elaborated.

"Yes," I said quickly. "I tracked down all those people myself, and I talked to them myself. I have the transcripts. Is everything okay?"

There was a pause on the other end of the line, then Ellen's voice, lighter and friendlier now, returned.

"Everything is great. You did an incredible job. I hope you'll be up for doing it again," she said. I had just earned twice my rent check in only ten days; I told her I was more than happy to do it whenever she wanted.

Over the next nine months, my life had two focuses. There were write-arounds for *Good Housekeeping*, which only grew more frequent after the Kathie Lee cover sold fantastically. I talked to friends of Sandra Bullock for an April *Good Housekeeping* cover, then it was Meg Ryan for June. A romance roundup for the February issue meant tracking down anyone I could find to talk about Barbra Streisand and James Brolin, as well as Will Smith and Jada Pinkett plus three other couples.

Meanwhile, back at my day job, it seemed as though hardly a week went by without several items about the "Portly Pepperpot." Technically, the Lewinsky scandal was over: Clinton had survived impeachment, and Monica had moved on to become a spokesperson for Jenny Craig, and a handbag designer. But that didn't mean that Page Six was going to leave her alone. Which is why one afternoon, I wrote an item whose sole purpose was to point out that Monica, still struggling with her weight, had moved into a new building in the Village...which had a bakery on its ground floor. I called the bakery's owner solely to ask if Monica had bought anything there yet and, if so, how caloric the items had been. The owner said Monica hadn't stopped in but added she was welcome anytime. In the item, I said the owner was "amused" at the thought of Monica coming in to "indulge" in croissants. An hour after I filed the story, I called my mother.

"Mom," I said. "I basically just wrote an item that goes: Monica Lewinsky is such a big fat fatty that she's definitely going to wind up bingeing at a bakery."

"I'm sure that's not what you wrote," my mom said reassuringly. I wasn't so certain. More and more, items about Monica seemed to have no purpose other than to point out all the ways in which she was still a fat, miserable failure. I knew that in the big picture, these little stories were probably just one small ping amid the white noise that had become the coverage of Monica. But they were striking a nerve with me nonetheless.

When I'd been in my second year at Oxford, and Clinton was in his second year as president, he'd come to visit the university, where he'd been a Rhodes Scholar. He asked to meet with all the current Rhodes Scholars, as well as any full-time American undergraduates, which included me. We met for tea on the lawn of the Rhodes building, and Clinton arrived with Hillary, several Secret Service staffers, and his press secretary, George Stephanopoulos. He gave a short speech in which he thanked us all for voting, regardless of whom we might vote for—"Apathy is a luxury that democracy cannot afford," he said—then went along a receiving line with Hillary and shook everyone's hand. I was one of the first people in the line, and as he shook my hand, he made direct eye contact and thanked me for coming to the reception.

"No, sir, thank you for what you're doing for our country," I managed to stammer.

"I'm going to do the very best that I can. I promise you that," he replied, still maintaining eye contact and, in my memory at least, doing that earnest-lip-bite thing that got parodied so much on *Saturday Night Live*.

I'm not gonna lie. If the next thing he'd said had been "Would you like a private tour of Air Force One? And my pants?" I would've said yes. To both.

Add to that the fact that I, too, knew all too well what it was like to struggle with a lingering freshman 15 (or 20, or even 25) weight gain, and I couldn't help but feel a connection to Monica. Yet at least once a week, for millions of readers, I mocked her. For her hair, her thighs, her assumed stupidity. Overwhelmed with guilt one evening, I found myself on the website for Monica's handbag collection, where I promptly spent an absurd amount of money for a tapestry-style tote bag emblazoned with a label that said MADE ESPECIALLY FOR YOU BY MONICA. I never brought it to work, and I still very much loved my job. But I was beginning to wonder about just how many shades of gray my soul had turned.

A month later, the phone rang and it was once again Ellen. Joanna was leaving, and I was being offered her job. It was a senior editor position, and I had never edited anything, anywhere, at all. Taking the job would catapult me over easily half a dozen years of paying my dues as assistant editor, associate editor, and staff editor. Then Ellen quoted me a salary that was more than twice what I was currently making. Finally, she proved why she is known industry-wide as a woman whom you should never, ever underestimate.

"The only condition is that you need to answer right now. I need to know by the end of this phone call," Ellen said.

It was a brilliant move; something in her tone made me know better than to argue that I needed more time, and by not giving it to me, she eliminated my ability to second-guess the offer, demand more money, or get cold feet.

Leaving the *Post*, however, would be incredibly painful if I chose to do it. It was my first real job, and the first real job I had truly loved. It made me forever abandon a desire to work for the *New Yorker* and instead taught me to embrace my inner tabloid warrior. It introduced me to newsroom culture, to working with people who mean what they say and who get things done fast while still getting them done right. It taught me that the words "celebrity journalist" are not an oxymoron. There was no artifice and no pretense, and there was a level of talent that I have only rarely encountered elsewhere. Still holding the phone with Ellen on the other line, I looked at the desks surrounding me. The mere thought of not seeing Jeane, or Richard, every day made me feel weepy. And for what: *Good Housekeeping*? A magazine read by middle-aged housewives? A magazine that no one I knew would purchase in a million years? I had power—albeit a somewhat twisted form—at Page Six. I loved the people I worked with, and most days, I loved what went into the column.

And yet. Here's an excerpt from an item that ran about Monica Lewinsky later that same year:

> An exclusive *Post* photo taken late last month shows the Portly Pepperpot has started living up to that nickname again.
>
> In recent sightings in her Greenwich Village neighborhood, Lewinsky appears to have put on some of the weight she dropped on the Jenny Craig program last year.
>
> She was even spotted munching on a bag of potato chips—definitely not allowed on the diet—as she waddled out of a D'Agostino's supermarket recently...
>
> "She seems awfully wide in the hips, and you can tell she has a double chin," one witness said.

At least I can say I didn't write that one. By that point, I was six months into my job as the Entertainment Editor at *Good Housekeeeping*. On my first day, I brought in several personal items, including the issue of Page Six in which my byline had first appeared and my *New York Post* coffee mug. I carried them all in my Monica Lewinsky tote bag.

The Four Most Absurd Celebrity Nicknames
Used While I Was at the *New York Post*

Why use someone's name when you can come up with a catchy moniker that could haunt them for years?

1. **The Portly Pepperpot.** For Monica Lewinsky. Obviously. This apparently was first suggested by a sportswriter at the paper, though that's been disputed. Over the years, multiple people have asked me just what the hell a Pepperpot is, anyway. It is either a bold and assertive person who acts outside social norms…or a spicy West Indian soup. The *Post* never used it without putting "Portly" in front of it, just in case anyone might forget that Monica wasn't thin.

2. **The Sultry Songbird.** This one was applied most often to Mariah Carey, who during my time at the *Post* was experiencing her post–Tommy Mottola break-up *Rumspringa*, sewing her wild oats with the likes of Derek Jeter. Every single time we wrote about her latest dalliance, this moniker would appear.

3. **The Bloviator.** For Alec Baldwin. His anger at the general persecution of Bill Clinton climaxed with a 1998 appearance on Conan O'Brien's *Late Night* show, where he screamed that if the US were a less civilized country, its citizens would rise up and "stone Henry Hyde to death." (Hyde was the Republican congressman who had a leadership role during the impeachment trial

of Clinton; he also later admitted to having had his own extramarital affair.) The *New York Post* is a solidly right-leaning paper, so comments like Baldwin's were not taken lightly. But in the grand tradition of "Portly Pepperpot" the ideal nickname is slightly ornate and antiquated. Hence, The Bloviator, a term used to signify a generally hot-winded orator. The word has had a bit of a resurgence lately as Donald Trump is sometimes called the "billionaire bloviator"—though never, ever in the *Post*.

4. **The Dusky Diva.** For Naomi Campbell. I cringe even to type the words, for obvious reasons. We wrote about her tantrums and misdeeds frequently at Page Six. I'm sorry to say, we used that phrase many, many times when we did.

Chapter 2

Jennifer Lopez Loves My Mother

DEPENDING ON HOW YOU DO THE MATH, A MONTHLY magazine like *Good Housekeeping* takes anywhere from three weeks to six months to produce. There are the weeks that immediately follow the closing of one issue and before the deadline of the next, roughly twenty-one days in which layouts need to be finalized, photos fine-tuned, and clever headlines conceived. But long before those details are hammered out, sometimes half a year or more before, big decisions need to be made. The biggest of these, of course, is who will be on the cover. The cover is the poster for the entire magazine, and no matter how good the chicken recipes or easy at-home workouts elsewhere in the issue might be, it's that smiling, celebrity face that carries the biggest burden for selling the issue.

Perhaps not surprisingly, stars were not clamoring to be on the cover of *Good Housekeeping*. It didn't matter that the magazine boasted twenty-six million readers, and that it reached more of the movie-going world than *Vanity Fair* ever would. As I settled into my new job at *GH*—I liked to use the acronym whenever possible so I wouldn't be reminded that I worked at a title that predated the suffrage movement—I learned that my role, from booking the all-important cover celebrity to helping arrange the photo shoot to, often, conducting the interview myself, was multifaceted. But all of the facets had one common aspect: begging.

Acronym or not, there was nothing sexy about *GH*, and at the turn of the millennium, the sort of stars *GH* wanted most for its cover—Reese Witherspoon, Jennifer Aniston, Meg Ryan, Sandra Bullock—wanted nothing to do with a title that conjured up images of happy 1950s homemakers in twinsets and pearls. During my days at Page Six, publicists had raced to take my calls; a high-powered representative for an A-list actor once said as she picked up, unaware that her assistant had already taken me off hold, "I need to take this; whenever this bitch calls it's either awful or amazing news." Now that I was at *GH*, publicists had no reason to fear me or placate me. Instead, they ignored me.

In the first year or so that I was at the magazine, I sent countless e-mails (and sometimes even faxes) in which I extolled the virtues of reaching twenty-six million readers, pointed out that we were a safe haven that wouldn't ask embarrassing questions, and finally—the pièce de résistance in dealing with time-crunched stars—that we needed just one hour of a celebrity's time. In other words, I begged. I begged to take publicists out for coffee when I was in LA, begged them to take my calls when I was back in New York, begged them to please just look at the "fun and fresh" things we were doing at the magazine. It felt as though I sent a new plea to a new person almost hourly. I came to intimately understand the line in *Jerry Maguire*, in which Jerry describes his job as "an up-at-dawn pride-swallowing siege that I will never fully tell you about," as I largely didn't tell Ellen about my elaborate system of bartering ("I'll feature *three* of your C-list stars for *one* of your A-listers!") and even more begging ("I am *imploring* you to please just consider what twenty-six million readers could do for her film."). The first five hundred times I begged I got nowhere. But somewhere around the 501st attempt, I started to break through. A sea change occurred after I got Madonna to agree to be on the cover to discuss her upcoming film *The Next Best Thing*. (Don't remember it? That's okay; she probably would rather you didn't.) Soon, other notable names followed suit, and every time an A-lister like Nicole Kidman said yes, it helped me lure another one for the following month.

Getting used to constant begging was only one part of my adjustment to life at *GH*. Almost as much of an adjustment was working with the other *GH* editors—most of whom were decades older than I was. While all of them were perfectly welcoming to the twentysomething now in their midst, I could tell Ellen herself was somewhat thrown by my relative youth when she first laid eyes on me after having only dealt with me over the phone. I sensed, from a few of her questions about my college years, that she was trying to ascertain just how old I was, but I figured it would only take a quick trip to Human Resources for her to find out for certain. Maybe she would have gone that route eventually. But then Rosie O'Donnell stepped in and saved her the trouble.

Only a few weeks after I started at *GH*, Rosie—then still beloved as the daytime talk show host dubbed "The Queen of Nice" by *Newsweek* magazine—was a guest judge at a recipe contest the magazine was holding in partnership with the Newman's Own line of foods. Contestants had to create a camp-out-appropriate recipe using one or more Newman's Own products, and the finalists were brought to New York for a taste-off judged by Rosie and a few other experts, including Tony Randall. (Decades later and I still have no idea how Tony Randall got involved.) Ellen brought me with her to the luncheon where the winner was to be decided.

Here's a quick example of Ellen Levine's inherent classiness: as she introduced me around the hotel dining room where the contest was being judged, she repeatedly said either, "This is Kate Coyne, the new entertainment editor who is working with me" or "This is the magazine's new Entertainment Editor, Kate Coyne. We're working together now." I was working *with* her, or we were working *together*—she never said I was working *for* her. Of course, I knew the truth: I was absolutely working *for* Ellen Levine. But she would never have phrased it that way, and a little thing like that made a huge difference to me as I tried to find my footing at the magazine.

I saw Rosie moving around the room, and Ellen swiftly steered me over to her. As Ellen made the introductions, Rosie made no secret of scanning me up and down.

"Hi," I said, offering my hand to her.

"Oh my god," she said. "You look like someone I should be babysitting. How old are you?"

I laughed and tried to treat the question as rhetorical.

"Oh, I'm older than I look, I guess..." I said and started to ask about the recipes she'd judged.

"Screw the recipes," Rosie said, cutting me off. "How old are you? I mean it: You look like some child. Seriously. How. Old. Are. You?"

I looked at Ellen, who seemed to be waiting avidly for the answer as well.

"Um..." I started. "I'm twenty-four."

"Oh Jesus," Rosie groaned. "Get away from me. You're a *baby*. Ellen, it's great seeing you." She gave Ellen a hug and headed back to the judging table. I finally made eye contact with Ellen and saw that both of her eyebrows were slightly raised.

In the cab back to the office afterward, and following ten minutes of discussion about upcoming stories, Ellen finally turned and looked at me.

"I assumed you were twenty-seven at least," she said.

I couldn't think of anything to say. I stared at my lap and half-shrugged.

"So, you're still a kid," Ellen said at last. "Well, then, I'm going to have to take good care of you."

She was true to her word. I might have already had my first great boss in Richard, but I now had my first great mentor. Ellen was herself a former protégée of Helen Gurley Brown's and was the first female editor of *Good Housekeeping*. She would wind up influencing everything from the way I dressed

(I'm convinced she invented the "statement necklace") to the men I dated (married since her early twenties, she and her husband, the dashing Dr. Richard Levine, had the sort of flirtatious banter after decades together that gave me hope for a similar happily-ever-after). But in my first year at *GH*, I still had a lot to learn.

When it came to snagging stars for the cover, there would always be certain celebrities who were what we called low-hanging fruit: obvious choices to whom our audience could relate. They were actresses of a certain age, often married, always with one or two kids, who could reliably be counted on to sell magazines. They weren't always the sexiest choices, but the fact remained that a cover featuring Joan Lunden and the twins she had via surrogate at age fifty-two started to feel pretty sexy when the sales numbers were through the roof.

But on the other end of the spectrum were the risks. Stars who weren't that well known but who had compelling stories to tell—like Charlize Theron, who was four years away from an Oscar but was starting to break through in a few hit movies and had survived childhood tragedy. Or a soap opera actress who nabbed the plum job as cohost of a beloved morning talk show, a woman named Kelly Ripa, whose hilarious anecdotes and girl-next-door charm were enough to override the fact that she had only just landed her gig on *Live! with Regis and Kelly* when I successfully pleaded with Ellen to put her on the cover. Or the TV star Jennifer Garner, at the time best known for the show *Alias*, whom we put on the cover when she was promoting her upcoming film *13 Going on 30* and after she had appeared in the superhero film *Daredevil* with Ben Affleck. We took on these riskier prospects at *Good Housekeeping* because often, taking a gamble on a star on her way up was the best shot we had at getting them at all. Established stars like Meg Ryan and Jennifer Aniston continued to think of themselves as "the wrong fit" (the excuse given by their publicists) for *Good Housekeeping*. I could only hope that actresses still ascending would remember that *GH* had given them a cover when many others hadn't wanted them yet and that they'd return to the magazine once they became huge. Some actually did (thank you, Kelly!). Eventually, after many years of my begging, even some well-known mega-stars would see the benefit of reaching such a vast audience: Reese Witherspoon did the cover to promote *Walk the Line*. Sandra Bullock, Julia Roberts, Meryl Streep all did it, as well. Even Meg finally came around. (No, Jennifer Aniston never did. Yes, I'm still cranky about that.)

The pleading never really stopped, though. I understood that if I began to get complacent, any ground I'd gained with publicists would quickly be lost. I exploited every possible angle when it came to badgering them. A newlywed celebrity was now a wife—and wives were *GH* readers. A star announcing a pregnancy was now on her way to being a mother—and moms were *GH* readers. A star divorcing was now going to be single and starting over—and so were many *GH* readers. There was no life angle I wasn't willing to exploit and every now and then an especially powerful piece of bait would become available: the possibility of redemption.

Stars coming off any sort of a scandal were prime targets for my cover pitch. There could be no safer, more wholesome place than *Good Housekeeping*, no better platform to show the world that you were an upstanding, moral, decent citizen of the world. Sometimes a scandal wasn't even necessary: as with Madonna, any star looking to add legitimacy to their image, or to appeal to a wider, more mainstream audience, was urged to seriously consider *Good Housekeeping*. If nothing else, I made sure that when publicists thought "mass-appeal," they thought *GH*.

By 2001, Jennifer Lopez was arguably the biggest star in the world. She'd just become the only person to have the number-one movie and the number-one album in America at the same time, as her film *The Wedding Planner* was a smash hit at the exact moment her album *J.Lo* topped the charts. She had also already weathered her fair share of tabloid headlines, mostly revolving around her romance with music mogul Sean Combs, who at the time went by the name "Puffy" or "Puff Daddy." (Later it became "P. Diddy" and after that "Diddy" and I won't even try to guess what it is now because it will likely have changed by the time I'm done with this sentence.) The two had been exiting a New York City nightclub when a shooting occurred, injuring three people; both stars were arrested for fleeing the scene in a Lincoln Navigator with a gun in the trunk. Jennifer was eventually released and never charged; Puffy was acquitted in the end. Not long after that, Jennifer proudly attended the Grammys with Puffy… and wore a green jungle-print Versace gown with a neckline that plunged down to her navel. It was the most famous celebrity dress moment since Marilyn Monroe stepped on a subway grate. Eventually, Jennifer and Puffy went their separate ways. The image of Jennifer as a bit of a bad girl, however, with a flair for high-risk romance—and super-risqué fashion—still lingered. A startlingly fast marriage to one of her back-up dancers, Cris Judd, only a few months after they were first linked as an item, didn't help. "Wholesome" and "old-fashioned" were not exactly words people were using to describe Jennifer Lopez. They were exactly the words people infuriatingly kept using to describe *Good Housekeeping*.

Granted, by spring of 2002, Jennifer Lopez didn't have much reason to care about whether people found her wholesome. What she did have was a new movie coming out, *Enough*, in which she was playing a wife and mother who seeks revenge after being abused by her husband. The studio hoped the movie would resonate with moms across America—the very people *GH* spoke to every month. I began badgering the studio to consider us as part of their press plan, but knew it wouldn't ultimately be their decision. Personal publicists are the true gatekeepers who determine which media requests will be approved. They are also the ones who care less about facts like readership numbers and more about what best suits their client's image and stature. When it came to Jennifer's publicist, I had really only one hope.

Good Housekeeping had a long history of supporting a domestic-violence victims organization called Safe Horizon, a group that had begun in Jennifer's native New York City. We had recently commissioned a profile on the work they did to help families in crisis, but it hadn't run yet. I realized that a Jennifer cover story timed to the release of *Enough* could be paired with the Safe Horizon story, which could run as a lengthy sidebar accompanying Jennifer's interview. I told her publicist to consider that doing a *GH* interview would practically be like issuing a public service announcement on behalf of abuse victims. "She could be helping so many people," I pleaded in an e-mail to her representative. In many ways, landing a star for a magazine cover is a lot like dating. You can't appear too needy or desperate, or it will be a turnoff. Hence, after my initial pleas, I would lie low for a week or so, at least, before following up. After e-mailing my Safe Horizon partnership idea to Jennifer's rep, I assumed I would get the same response I normally got when trying to wrangle a star generally considered too good for *GH*: silence. That silence, by the way, means the exact same thing as the silence that follows a date: thanks, but no thanks.

So I was stunned when just four days after my e-mail, Jennifer's publicist called. The Safe Horizon angle intrigued Jennifer, he said. Furthermore, the magazine felt like a good fit for this particular film. Jennifer was in. I muffled a victory whoop before I hung up and then openly shrieked in my office. By that point, two years into my time at *GH*, nabbing Jennifer was hands down my biggest celebrity "get." Now I only needed to make sure Ellen—who had told me to go ahead and offer the cover but, like me, had little expectation it would actually happen—was as enthusiastic as I was.

Understandably, Ellen's enthusiasm was tempered with some caution, and concern. Jennifer Lopez, wearer of that Versace dress, wouldn't quite sit right with some of *GH*'s more conservative readers.

"What's the problem? Clearly she's conservative, too: She keeps getting married! She believes in holy matrimony! She's Catholic!" I protested, only partially kidding.

Then Ellen asked the make-or-break question for any celebrity being considered for any magazine, anywhere.

"What's the line?" she said, and raised an eyebrow.

Remember how I said a celebrity's smiling face was the most important part of a magazine cover? I was partially wrong. Equally important are the great big words that run right underneath her face: what's known as the coverline, or simply the line. Without breaking news—monthly magazines work too far in advance to ever be able to capitalize on that—an entire category of promotion is eliminated. No "Divorce Shocker!" or "Her Secret Heartbreak." By the time a monthly magazine hits stands three months after going to press, you can't rely on a secret or shock left to reveal. So for a magazine like *GH* especially, it wasn't enough to land a star for the cover; we had to know what sort of story she was going to be telling, and most of all, how to succinctly sell that story, usually in no more than four or five words. Obviously, this limits options considerably. There's a reason you'll see the same few phrases again and again. Star diagnosed with cancer? "My Brave Battle" or "I'm Going to Beat This." Star who has now beaten cancer or some other brush with death? "I'm Lucky to Be Alive." Star who has finally found happiness after a string of bad marriages or break-ups? "How Love Saved Me" or, most obvious of all, "Happy At Last." Then there's the "From...To" construct, always useful in conveying someone's entire life journey with an economy of words: "From Tears to Triumph" or "From Heartbreak to Happiness." When all else fails, there are the super-general lines that mean everything while saying nothing: "My Own Story," "My Side of The Story," "My Turn to Talk."

Now Ellen, whose regal bearing still had the power to slightly terrify me, wanted to know what my Jennifer line would be. In some ways, it's an impossible question to answer before an interview has taken place: how can anyone know if she'll be defiant or emotional or witty? Still, it remains crucial to have at least an idea of what you hope the line will be, so that you can ideally steer the interview in that direction. Given Ellen's rightful concern that our readers would be judgmental of J.Lo, I focused on a somewhat declarative tone.

" 'The Real Jennifer'?" I offered. Ellen looked unimpressed.

" 'The Truth about Me'?" I kept going, sensing I was getting warmer.

" 'What You Don't Know about Me'?" I said next.

"And what is it we want people to know about her?" Ellen said.

I thought for a moment. A few weeks earlier, VH1 had aired a documentary on Jennifer's climb. Hoping we might get her for the magazine by that point, I had watched avidly. The special charted her life from a working-class section of the Bronx where she attended Catholic school with her two sisters, through lean years as a dancer, to bit parts where her work ethic and dynamic presence made her a standout. Every single person interviewed on the show raved about her tirelessness and determination. More than one commented on her true love of performing. And several mentioned her devotion to her family and her roots. There wasn't a single trace of diva-like antics or demanding bitchery. That was the Jennifer I wanted *GH* readers to know.

"I guess I want them to know that . . . she's good, you know? That she's not some bad girl. That she's actually a good girl," I stammered to Ellen.

"So that would be the line? *She's a good girl?*" Ellen said, arching one eyebrow, dubious.

"N-n-no," I stammered. "But maybe like a quote from her? 'I *Am* a Good Girl.' And we could italicize the 'am' for emphasis."

"I *am* a good girl," Ellen repeated to herself. She was silent for a minute, considering it.

"Okay," she said finally. "That could work. That could be good."

I smiled triumphantly.

"Good luck getting her to say it," Ellen added.

Somehow, I managed to keep my smile intact. But I had just learned an important lesson. Getting the "yes" had seemed like it would be the hardest part of my job, and at Page Six, it had been pretty much the only part. Get the item, get the quote, get it in the column. It was all about the get. But now, at *Good Housekeeping*, I was having to figure out how best to package what I had gotten. I had to go beyond the "get" and also think about the "sell." It wasn't enough to make Jennifer Lopez say yes to *Good Housekeeping*; now I had to figure out how to make *Good Housekeeping* readers say yes to Jennifer Lopez. Telling them what a nice, sweet, good girl she was seemed like as good an approach as any.

Two weeks later plans were in place for me to fly to Los Angeles and interview Jennifer at the production offices she kept there. It wasn't until the night before that I began to truly feel anxious. Just as I was packing, my mother called.

"Are you wearing red underwear tomorrow?" she asked because she has a strange obsession with my clothes. Actually, no, she doesn't, she just has a mid-grade fear of flying that she assuages in part by believing in certain superstitions. The red underwear one, in fact, came courtesy of Ellen, who had once told me it was good luck to wear red underwear when flying. I mentioned it to my mom, who promptly seized it as gospel truth and now insisted upon my wearing red underwear when I flew. My mother, in fact, adored Ellen, though they'd only briefly met once. Still, after watching me run around New York swigging champagne on behalf of Page Six, Mom was hugely relieved to see me land at a reputable magazine under the wing of someone as venerable as Ellen.

"Yes, I'm wearing it," I said with a sigh. "But that's seriously the least of my worries right now."

"The least of your worries is your plane falling from the sky?" my mother said. "I really don't know what could top that, worry-wise."

"Worrying won't stop my plane from falling out of the sky," I said. "So I might as well worry about something else, which is how to make Jennifer Lopez say a ridiculously specific sentence."

"Why, what exactly do you need her to say?" my mom asked.

"I *am* a good girl," I replied.

"Yes, you are. You are my very own good, sweet girl. And I'm sure you'll be able to get Jennifer Lopez to say what you want her to say. So what is the sentence?" my mom said, as we edged dangerously close to a bad rendition of "Who's on First?"

"No, Mom, that's the sentence. I have to get Jennifer Lopez to say 'I am a good girl.' No, not even: she has to say it, like, 'I *am* a good girl,' emphasis on *am*, sort of like she's declaring it to all her detractors or something: I *am* a good girl!"

I heard myself saying it out loud and suddenly felt even more absurd.

"Hmmmm…" my mother said, pondering my predicament. "Well, honey, you know, is she really *that* good? I mean there was that thing with that Fluffy person and…"

"No! Mom!" I said, suddenly feeling defensive of a woman I had yet to meet. "Listen, did you know her mother worked two jobs, and she and her two sisters went to Catholic school and church every Sunday, and she went to every single dance class her parents could scrape together money for, and she's like a really devoted daughter and sister?"

I knew exactly the chord this would strike with my mom. My mother was supposed to be the next Shirley Temple. Enrolled in dance classes almost as soon as she could walk, she was a tap-dancing, back-flipping child star who never quite found mega-stardom, but did land on *The Mickey Mouse Club* and won countless talent competitions, several thanks to a number she did in a grass skirt called "When Hilo Hattie Does the Hilo Hop." She managed all this despite the last name Druckenbrod (which was never changed to a stage name, but which she happily abandoned when she married my dad). By the time she was a teen, the superstardom hopes had been abandoned; instead, in adulthood she settled for starting and successfully running the largest theatrical advertising agency on Broadway. Suffice it to say, Ellen Levine wasn't the first formidable woman I'd encountered: I was raised by one. At my swanky private school on Manhattan's Upper East Side, my mom was one of two working mothers in my entire class. Hearing about how Jennifer had taken dance lessons and was good to her working mom was a surefire way to win my mother over.

"Okay, I totally think you can say she's a good girl," my mom said now, fully convinced.

"Yeah, Mom, I know, that's not the problem; it's how to get *her* to say it . . ."

"Well, you know what, even if she doesn't say it, you tell her from me that your own nice mommy knows what a good girl she is. I'm sure she'll appreciate hearing that," my mom offered finally.

This was almost a running joke between us; whenever I was having trouble booking a celebrity for a cover, my mother would semi-seriously recommend a Broadway star. "Betty Buckley is coming back to *Cats*! You could do her!" she'd say, or "Don't you want to put Patti LuPone on your cover? She's going to be great in *Gypsy*!" Finally, when I'd brush off all her suggestions, she'd say, "Okay, fine, I'll do it. Just put your own nice mommy on the cover." So to suggest I bring "my own nice mommy" up in conversation with Jennifer Lopez wasn't exactly a novel suggestion for her.

"Okay, Mom, thanks. I'll do that," I said and returned to packing.

Two days later, I was sitting in the reception area of Nuyorican Productions, the film production company Jennifer ran out of Los Angeles. While I waited for Jennifer to be ready for me, her publicist came out to chat. An incredibly decent and nice guy, Jennifer's rep at the time was a sort of old-school publicist who still did business in a straightforward and direct manner. A newer wave of publicists now saw themselves as a hybrid of bodyguard and curator, tightly controlling their client's image and often seeking to spin and obscure anything that didn't fit that facade, even if it meant lying to the press.

But Jennifer's publicist was more traditional: he saw his job as fielding requests for his client and making sure she was treated fairly. Sitting next to me in the waiting area, he didn't bombard me with rules and restrictions on what I could or couldn't say, or what I was forbidden to ask. I liked him instantly. As we sat chatting, he mentioned that Jennifer was running behind schedule that day because she was still filming a new movie.

"Oh, which one?" I asked him.

"It's called *Gigli*. It's costarring Ben Affleck. I think it's gonna be great. And she'll be a great influence on Ben," he added, notable since Ben had not long before gone into rehab. "They're great together."

Of course, Jennifer was still married to Cris Judd, so I barely gave the comment much thought. Moments later, Jennifer, wearing a velour sweatsuit, no makeup, diamond studs the size of dimes on her ears, and her hair pulled back in a bun, opened the door to her office and invited me in.

She was absolutely radiant, but also completely approachable. I had worried that the "diva reputation" would somehow be in effect, and make her seem cold or distant. Instead, she kicked off her shoes and plopped down cross-legged on the couch.

"What can I get you? You need water or anything?" she asked earnestly. I declined as I began to realize that I was still nervous enough that there was a decent chance I would somehow spill water on myself if given the opportunity.

We began talking about her journey to stardom, and her role in *Enough*. Jennifer knew how to deliver a good anecdote, and made several references to having suffered "emotional abuse" in a previous relationship. Especially in light of her past with Puffy, it was the kind of statement that was certain to get quoted in the press and on entertainment shows once it appeared in *GH*, and I was inwardly thrilled when she said it. But she wasn't purely slick and polished, either. I noticed she'd end every third or fourth sentence with the phrase "You know what I mean?" strung together almost like one long exhale: "YouknowwhatImean?" It was actually pretty endearing, and showed just how much she was trying to deliver a relatable message to our readership, to be seen and heard for who she really was.

But I was still nowhere near getting her to declare herself a good girl.

I asked about her marriage, and I found it only slightly suspicious that she kept referring to her husband in the past tense.

"At the time that I met Cris, that love was very healing," she said, obliquely referencing her breakup from Puffy. "In the midst of this crazy storm that is my life, that love was what I needed most of all. And he filled that void for me."

After talking for a while about her wedding to Cris just four days after the events of 9/11, and her plans for kids "someday," I began to cautiously steer the conversation back toward the fallout from her relationship with Puffy, and how the media had often portrayed her as relentlessly fame-hungry. Here was my glimmer of hope, my chance that she would address her critics.

"People mistake having a dream for being abnormally ambitious, and it's not about that," she said. "I'm like, 'Excuse me for having a dream since the day I was born!'"

She shrugged, and offered no further defense. I glanced at my watch and realized that my hour was almost over. I began to frantically think of what else I could say.

"You know VH1 ran a documentary special on you," I suddenly announced. Jennifer's eyes widened; she was aware of the special.

"Oh, no, you watched it?" she asked. I told her I had and she groaned.

"Oh that was so traumatic!" she said with a laugh. "My husband and my friend Arlene and everyone watched it, and they were just enjoying every minute of it . . . still, for me." She shuddered dramatically.

I laughed, too, but the voice in my head was chanting: *"I* am *a good girl. I* am *a good girl. I* am *a good girl. Say it say it say it say it."*

"I'm really glad I got a chance to watch that, though, because I feel like I saw a side of you that most people probably don't know about," I said eagerly.

Jennifer just shrugged and rolled her eyes, clearly still bemused by the photos that the special had dredged up. This wasn't working. She wasn't anywhere near defiant or attempting to set the record straight.

"But, *come on*," I said, a little too emphatically. "I think more people *should* know about the real you. About how your background and your work ethic and your beginnings helped shape you. Don't you feel like sometimes you wish more people knew that about you? That you're not just the gorgeous, glamorous movie star but also a good girl from that street in the Bronx?"

There. I had practically said it for her. Repeat after me,

Jennifer: I *am* a good girl. (I also realize now I should probably take credit for inspiring her to later write "Jenny from the Block." You're welcome, America.)

Jennifer nodded her head slightly. "There's this misconception that when women work hard and go after what they want, there has to be some evil side to their personality, which I think is so unfair," she said. Then she smiled again and just looked at me. The interview time was nearly over.

My mind raced. What could I say? What would help here? One final option came to me.

"You know who loves you since that VH1 thing?" I blurted out. "My mother. I told my mom all about it. And she just *loooooves* you. She told me to tell you that you shouldn't care about what anyone else thinks of you: she's a mother, and she can tell that you're a good girl. She told me to tell you that. She knows you're a good girl."

I prayed I didn't look as desperate as I sounded. Jennifer furrowed her brow for a minute, and my heart stopped. She thought I was ridiculous, clearly.

Then she broke into a huge grin.

"Aww, you know what, only a mother would be able to tell that," she said. "Tell your mom I said thank you."

She was silent for another minute and just as I began to fear the worst, she sat up a little straighter and spoke with renewed conviction.

"And you know what? Why do I have to be *bad* because I'm successful? How about *because* I'm good, I've been able to become successful? I especially think if you're sensual or attractive, people want to think the worst of you for some reason. But you know what, I'm going to go out on a limb and say I *am* a good girl. I am. And this other image of me—there's nothing further from the truth."

It was all I could do not to shout with glee. I leapt to my feet; whether the interview was officially over or not, I knew it wasn't going to get any better. She said it. *She said it, she said it, she said it.*

"Thank you so much," I said, grateful in ways she couldn't have realized. If she had offered a hug, I probably would have crushed her to death. Instead, she held out a perfectly manicured hand. I shook it and practically raced out of her office, terrified that she was suddenly going to stop me and say, "Don't repeat what I said about being a good girl, you know what I mean?"

Twelve weeks later, there she was on the cover, gorgeous in a yellow dress, declaring "I *Am* a Good Girl." Jennifer's comments about having been in an emotionally abusive relationship got plenty of attention, as I'd known they would. As far as I was concerned, they paled in comparison to the five most important words in the whole interview. It's one of the finest quotes I've ever gotten. Just ask my own nice mommy.

Chapter 3

Mariska Hargitay Thinks I'm a Stalker

HERE'S THE PROBLEM WITH SPENDING NEARLY TWENTY years chronicling the minutiae of the rich and famous. When you know where Matt Damon's kids go to school and the type of hair dryer Meryl Streep prefers and the name of the lawyer that is on retainer by a certain A-list star convinced his marriage could end at any moment... it becomes hard not to feel as though you actually *know* these people, intimately. By that sort of logic, they must also, therefore, know you. Every year I attend various award ceremonies in Los Angeles. Every year, as Melissa McCarthy floats past me or Colin Firth saunters by, I have a brief moment, just a nanosecond, where I nearly reach out to them and say cheerfully, "Hey, Melissa! How are you! How is your house renovation coming along?"

That's when I have to listen to the little voice in my head that is frantically shouting, *"You don't know them! They don't know you! Do not go up to them!"*

It's being star-struck in reverse. You're falsely familiar, forgetting that knowing every last detail of what someone did on their summer vacation doesn't, in fact, mean they in turn know the first thing about you. Or, more importantly, that they would even care.

It's a lesson that's even harder to learn when you've actually interviewed and spent time with a celebrity, and she's gone out of her way to be friendly, warm, and engaging. That's right, Mariska Hargitay. I'm looking at you.

I had been the Entertainment Editor at *Good Housekeeping* magazine for four years by the time *Law & Order: SVU* really took off. As *GH* had begun to establish itself more and more as a decent contender for a celebrity cover, a miraculous thing happened. Every now and then a publicist would actually approach me and ask me to consider a client. The thrill of a bird in the hand was almost too good to overlook, so unless the client was someone truly unknown or past their peak, I would almost always try to see if there was a way to make a cover work.

So when Mariska Hargitay's publicist called and pointed out that *Law & Order: SVU* was now a beloved and bona fide hit and that her client Mariska Hargitay was long overdue to be on the cover of a major magazine, I paid attention. I went to Ellen and made a case for Mariska. Only problem: Mariska's rep wanted the October cover, on stands in September, timed to the start of the new season of *SVU*. Yet traditionally, *GH* always had a solid newsstand sale by skipping a celebrity cover that month and running some sort of Halloween/Harvest cover featuring artfully carved pumpkins. Considering that it gave me a break from the ten other covers I had to beg for (December was another month off: we always ran the winner of a gingerbread house contest) I had never minded it. But now I had a celebrity who wanted October, and I had a preexisting commitment to some gourds.

"Talk to her rep and explain the pumpkin situation," Ellen said, in one of those sentences that made me wonder why I'd gone to college. Surely my extensive study of Keats and Shelley would now come in handy as I tried to explain "the pumpkin situation."

Mariska's rep didn't miss a beat.

"So she'll hold some pumpkins on the cover! She's happy to do that!" she said.

I could think of no reply. Amazingly, neither could Ellen.

So two weeks later, a very game and exceedingly lovely Mariska Hargitay did a photo shoot in which she posed with all manner of autumnal items. There were sunflowers, dried leaves, Indian corn, and pumpkins. So many pumpkins.

A week after that, I met Mariska at the bar at the Four Seasons Hotel in midtown Manhattan for our interview. Though *SVU* was indeed popular, this was several years before Mariska would win an Emmy for her portrayal of Detective Olivia Benson, and still before reruns of the show would begin airing around the clock. Back at the office, editors had been concerned that there might not be a way to make readers feel an emotional connection to someone still as relatively unknown as Mariska. Once again, the question was asked: What's the line? What are the words we can put on the cover that will sell this star? It was quickly decided that she needed to deliver some sort of emotional saga. Would she talk at length about the grisly car-accident death of her mother, the legendary bombshell Jayne Mansfield, which happened when Mariska was just three years old, and how that loss had irrevocably changed her? You know, just your typical, fun, fall cover story! Motherless daughters—what's more enjoyable than that? Other than being the lucky interviewer who gets to ask her all about it?

Of course, when I finally broached the somber topic with her, Mariska was a pro, and an incredibly kind and patient one at that. At the time, she was in the midst of planning her wedding. As a newlywed myself at that point, I eagerly ooh'ed and aah'ed as she showed me photos of her pale pink Carolina Herrera gown. She talked about how her husband-to-be, Peter, had proposed and how swept away she'd been in that moment, and about her long struggle to be taken seriously in Hollywood. "I walked into a lot of auditions where, because of my mom, people would look at me and say, 'Oh, I thought you'd be blonder.'" Mariska didn't hesitate to share the ways in which losing her mom continued to resonate with her. "I just always felt robbed," she said, choking up. "Everyone else in the world had such strong feelings about this woman that I should have known the best. But I never got to know her at all."

It was extraordinarily easy to be charmed by her, and to know she deserved every bit of success and stardom she could ever want. "Sometimes I can't believe I'm not a drug addict or alcoholic," she said, laughing through her tears at one point. "I would lapse into catastrophic thinking a lot, where I was just convinced the worst thing would happen. But I worked hard to stop those patterns, because I realized, if you think something's going to end badly, sweetheart, it will."

Mariska talked about her mom some more, and she cried several times throughout the two hours—mostly happy tears about the man she loved, and about her excitement for her future; she couldn't wait to have a family and was leaning toward the name "Isabella Jayne" if she ever had a girl. During the course of shedding those tears, she laughed at my various pop culture references, marveled at the random facts about her career I'd managed to retain—"You remember when I was on *Falcon Crest*?" she shrieked (and of course I did: her character was excellently named Carly Fixx)—and began to feel like an old friend. Spending time with a warm and friendly celebrity is a little like visiting a boyfriend in prison. No matter how much you may like them, there's a limit to just how cozy you're allowed to become. So even when it turns out that a star you're interviewing loves exactly the same films you do or is actively listening to the same album you have on your iPod at that very moment or attended the same summer camp you did, you can only let yourself get but so excited about it. Inwardly, I may be thinking, *Oh my god, it would be so great to get pumpkin spice lattes with you followed by mani-pedis*, but outwardly, I've got to keep that sentiment very much in check. Mariska

Hargitay probably gave me the biggest run for my money when it came to not revealing that I was rapidly developing a girl crush. (Kelly Ripa is a close second.) Particularly since Mariska seemed to be doing such a great job at reciprocating the sentiment. After I mentioned her short-lived buddy cop series *Tequila and Bonetti* (with a title like that, how could it have been canceled?), she audibly gasped and grabbed my arm.

"That's it. You have to come to game night at my house," she declared. "I have this big game of charades once a month, and we play guys against girls, and you have to come and be on my team. Your husband can play on Peter's team. We play with my best friend, Hilary, and her husband, Chad."

Those with a decent long-term memory and an obsession with celebrities will know that she meant Hilary Swank and her then-husband, Chad Lowe. I, of course, knew that instantly. I nodded and said, "Sure, I'd love to come." Then I silently added, *And maybe afterward we can get pumpkin spice lattes and mani-pedis.*

With that, Mariska was ripping out a piece of paper and pushing it toward me. "Will you write down your cell number? That way I'll know how to contact you? Oh, this will be so great! You'll be my secret weapon," she said happily.

I wrote down my number, signaled for the check, and thanked Mariska for her time. "No, thank *you*," she said warmly. "I really appreciate getting to do this with you guys." She was gracious and generous, and, best of all, she hugged me. You can tell a lot about how open a celebrity is willing to be based on whether or not, after two hours spent talking to you, they feel comfortable enough to give you a hug. Mariska Hargitay was a hugger, and I couldn't have been happier about it.

When I got home that night, I told my husband all about my new best friend.

"You will love her so much," I said. "She's gorgeous, but also so funny and sweet. And the guy she's marrying, Peter, is a jock just like you, and he loves sports and is a real guy's guy, and here's the best part: we are going to go over to her house to play charades with her and Hilary Swank and Chad Lowe!"

My husband, bless his heart, is frequently unsure who the hell I am talking about when I mention celebrities. Here's the type: if our television suddenly stopped getting the various sports networks, he would have virtually no use for it. For example, not long ago, while watching Wimbledon on television, we had an exchange that went like this:

"Kate, who was John McEnroe once married to?"

"Tatum O'Neal."

"Right, right. Wait, who was she again?"

"She's the actor Ryan O'Neal's daughter and she won an Oscar for *Paper Moon* when she was really young, and then she had some success as a teen actress, and then she grew up and became a total mess and has struggled off and on with addiction. She was married to McEnroe for about six years and had three kids with him. Sean, Emily, and Kevin. And then she was in that *Sex and the City* episode where she played Carrie's bitchy friend who lost her shoes." (This is where I should point out that those facts came right off the top of my head, including the names of Tatum and John's three kids. I am aware that this says something very sad about the state of my brain.)

"So...was she the actress I was asking you about the other day?" he asked.

"I don't think so. Who did you ask me about the other day?"

"You know...Leona Toni?"

"..."

It took me a minute to remember the conversation we'd had, and that it was about David Duchovny's ex-wife.

"Téa Leoni? Do you mean Téa Leoni when you say Leona Toni?"

"Yes! Téa Leoni! So, is that who McEnroe married?"

"Are you actually asking me if Tatum O'Neal is Téa Leoni, aka Leona Toni? Are you asking me if these are all the same person?"

"Yeah, I guess not."

So it wasn't really a surprise that while I squealed about playing charades with Mariska Hargitay, Hilary Swank, and Chad Lowe, he seemed largely unmoved.

"Okay, sounds nice," he said. "Just tell me when."

I shrugged. "I'm sure it will be any day now," I said confidently.

And yet.

As weeks became months, there was no call from Mariska. When the cover hit stands, featuring a radiant Mariska holding armfuls of sunflowers (which we, shockingly, had chosen over the pumpkins), I heard through her publicist that she was thrilled with the story and had loved meeting me. My cellphone still didn't ring. To make matters worse, whenever an episode of *SVU* would come on, my husband would turn to me with a smirk.

"Hey," he'd say without fail. "Aren't we supposed to be going over to her house to play charades?" After which I would usually punch some portion of his upper body.

Time passed. Lives changed. Hilary and Chad broke up—and my beloved spouse, not missing the opportunity, said in a fake-panic when he heard the news: "Wait, what are we going to do about charades now?" At which point I punched a portion of his lower body. Mariska eventually sold her amazing downtown apartment, and I'll admit to staring at the photos when they appeared online, imagining the festive game nights that must have taken place in her impeccably decorated living room. Then, five years after the cover story, I found myself in Los Angeles at a party celebrating that year's Emmy nominees.

Far better than attending award shows themselves—which, by the third time you do it, mostly means three hours spent in Spanx while you slowly starve—are the parties in the days that lead up to it. The celebrations consist of two portions: first, a small red carpet in front, where the celebrities attending a party hosted by any number of power players—a network or cable channel, a magazine or trade publication, a major talent agency—pose for pictures and give a handful of quotes to eager reporters waiting for the chance to ask them about either their award nomination (if the celeb is lucky enough to have received one) or whom they're rooting for at the awards (if they're not lucky enough to have received one). Second comes the jockeying, fawning, mingling, and generally organized gawking that occurs inside the party. Every celebrity has another celebrity they adore; when Brad and Angelina attended the after-party for the Screen Actors Guild (SAG) Awards, I witnessed two different mega-star actresses—one of whom had just won an award that night—nearly fall over themselves trying to get a glimpse of the couple. Very little from these parties ever makes it into print or online, beyond a description of what a star wore, or a new-couple alert if someone showed up with an interesting date. Breaking news is beside the point. Networking, connecting with publicists, and maybe, ideally, getting to sneak a few glimpses at a star you worship, are the main objectives.

The week that I was in Los Angeles, I found myself invited to a slew of parties so exclusive and starry that I frequently wondered if my name had only accidentally made it onto the guest list. As I clutched a glass of warm, half-sipped champagne, I would mostly stare in awe at the celebrities who wandered past me while I wondered if I could find the nerve to talk to any of them. One particular Friday night bash was exceptionally A-list: as Tina Fey walked past me, I managed a squeak that sounded like a mouse being strangled, which she, mercifully, didn't hear. I went to get a glass of champagne at the bar and found myself standing next to Jon Hamm, who gave me a very Don Draper–esque nod and half smile. I responded by sneezing loudly (note: he said, "Bless you") before scurrying away.

That's when I saw her. My old pal. Mariska.

Her publicist wasn't with her, but her friend Julianna

Margulies was. I had a dilemma. Should I really go up to her and reintroduce myself, knowing full well that in the ensuing years she had been on countless covers, interviewed innumerable times, had become a wife and mother and Emmy winner, and therefore had zero reason to remember me? Or should I come to my senses, stay put in the corner and simply finish my champagne?

I finished my champagne.

Then I walked over to Mariska and Julianna.

"Hey, Mariska, I'm sorry to bother you," I said, which is what every person says when they aren't at all sorry to have bothered you. She turned to me and cocked her head, which was all the encouragement I needed to keep going.

"My name is Kate Coyne and I don't expect you to remember this," I began, "but I interviewed you five years ago, for your first-ever cover story, for *Good Housekeeping*."

Mariska smiled warmly and said, "Of course! How are you?" but I should have noticed that there was no real glimmer of recognition in her eyes. Still, I plowed on, and began babbling congratulations for her Emmy nomination that year. She responded that she couldn't believe she'd been nominated at all considering that Glenn Close, then starring in *Damages*, was now in the running. But while she graciously praised Glenn and the other nominees, in my head, I began to think of what else I could say to her to make her recall our magical time together. Was there a specific moment from our lunch that would trigger her memory of how much she had loved me? Something that would spark a moment where she recognized me as the long-lost awesome girl she had been trying to track down all these years? I figured I could say something like this:

You know, Mariska, it's so funny, I'm sure you don't remember this, but when I interviewed you, you mentioned this big charades game night you do at your house. And you were so sweet, you actually said I should come and play sometime, even though obviously you were just being kind. But hilariously, I told my husband that you'd said that, and for the past four years, he's been teasing me every time he sees you on TV and saying, "When are we going to her house to play charades?" So I guess on his behalf what I should be asking you is, How come you never invited me over to play charades?

Here's the problem: I *thought* all of that in my head. But as Mariska and Julianna politely chatted with me while I nodded and smiled and rehearsed my speech inwardly, I became convinced that they knew exactly what I was thinking. Surely, we were all on the same page here! Surely, she remembered everything we had discussed all those years ago! Surely, she now had total recall of who I was! So while I had a thorough explanation planned in my head, I didn't *say* most of it out loud. I only said the last part. The very very last part.

"So, how come you never invited me over to play charades?" I suddenly demanded, seemingly out of nowhere.

Let's review, shall we? The last sentence she heard me say right before that one was "Congratulations on your Emmy nomination!" My conversation with her veered from "Congrats!" to "Why didn't you invite me over?" in about fifteen seconds. I'm fairly sure I gasped a little, audibly, when I realized what I had done. We were not on the same page. Not even close. I quickly realized saying more would probably not fix the problem. Words had gotten me into this mess, but it didn't seem likely that more words would get me back out. I silently counted down from five, willing Mariska to laugh by the time I reached zero.

Instead, a stunned Mariska looked over at Julianna, slightly panicked. "Excuse me?" she said, furrowing her exquisite brow.

I quickly switched tactics and hoped maybe more words would be my salvation after all. I began to chatter nervously, scrambling to make my tongue catch up to my brain.

"No, *nooo*," I practically mooed. "I was being funny, because, see, when I interviewed you, you said this thing about charades...you said I should play at your house, and Hilary and Chad would be there—and by the way, I'm sorry about that divorce; how is Hilary doing?—and anyway, I told my husband and now there's always this teasing, about the charades, see, because he's all, 'When are we playing charades with Mariska?' and so I thought it would be funny, you know, to ask about the charades but it's a joke! It's a charades joke! Like, why didn't you call me to play charades, *ha ha ha ha!*"

Then it happened: As I cackled like a lunatic, Mariska's gorgeous Louboutin stilettos took two steps backward. She was physically trying to get away from me. She was slowly backing away from the scary stalker that I had become. I thought about throwing some more words at her in hopes of making things right. Then I noticed she was also tightly clutching Julianna's hand. Probably squeezing out SOS in Morse code. I knew it was time to cut my losses.

"You ladies have a great evening," I said, emulating some sort of smooth grandpa. Who actually says things like "you ladies" anymore? Apparently I do. They both nodded at me and hurriedly turned away. I race-walked back to my dark corner and remained there for the rest of the evening.

———

About six months later, I was having lunch with a well-known producer, and I decided to see if maybe my own mortification had worn off enough to make the Mariska Incident, as I had begun calling it, at least a funny lunch story.

"So, I had this interesting thing happen with Mariska Hargitay in the week leading up to the Emmys..." I began.

"Oh my god, I love Mariska!" the producer exclaimed. "I've known her for years. She has this amazing game night at her house where we all play charades."

For a split-second I wondered if someone had put him up to this, had tipped him off. Then I realized the improbability of it.

"Wait... Jesus, why are you banging your head against the table?" the producer was soon shrieking at me. "Oh my god, stop!"

Since then, I have seen Mariska Hargitay at a dozen different Hollywood parties. One wintry afternoon in a park on the Upper West Side of Manhattan, I watched my kids playing with a beautiful long-eyelashed boy whom I thought I recognized... and then I realized I did, from a *Got Milk?* ad in which he posed smiling in the lap of his famous mom: Mariska Hargitay. A moment later, I spotted Mariska standing by the sandbox. I all but ran in the opposite direction.

What's more, in the past few years, I've been the editor of two stories on Mariska's adoption of a daughter as well as a second son. But I have never, ever spoken another word to her.

Still... Mariska, if you're reading this? I've never changed my number, and I'm sure you still have that piece of paper somewhere. Call me!

Chapter 4

Wynonna Judd Made Me Eat, Pray, and Love

NEARLY ALL CELEBRITY INTERVIEWS TAKE PLACE in one of two locations: a relatively quiet corner of a photo studio where a shoot has just taken place for the cover story, or a restaurant. There are, of course, exceptions: a hotel suite, or that rarest of events, a celebrity's actual home. But more often than not, talking to a star means either perching on a white slipcovered sofa that was earlier used in a photograph—they seem to almost always be white, so that the color can be changed after the fact to just about anything; it's not just the humans that get Photoshopped!—or ordering a mixed green salad with grilled chicken at some discreetly mid-scale restaurant where you hope your tape recording won't be drowned out by the sound of the silverware.

The majority of stars who schedule interviews over lunch or breakfast will barely pick at their plates over the course of an hour. I've found only one type of exception to this: if they are exceedingly beautiful and feminine, they will make a point of ordering the most calorie-laden item on the menu (such as the drop-dead gorgeous A-lister who requested corned beef hash topped with two poached eggs…and then ate it all) to hammer home the message that they're real women with real appetites and are not merely the wafer-thin constructs of their stylists and publicists. It is intended to be both disarming and charming, and I have to admit, it's hard not to like a woman who polishes off a mountain of meat at breakfast (hi, Charlize!).

As for my own food choices during these interviews, there are certain obvious rules. Anything involving slurping, swirling, or the use of chopsticks is out. Anything too labor-intensive, like sawing through a huge steak, is similarly forbidden. I generally try to mirror whatever the star has ordered without ordering exactly the same thing. You don't order a burrito if Reese Witherspoon has just ordered tea and toast. Of course, such dainty selections are hardly what I want to order, but that's not the point. I can probably count on one hand the number of times I have ever ordered exactly what I wanted at a restaurant. Because, truth be told, what I *want* to order is all the food. All of it.

I am capable of eating roughly as much as my husband, who played football for over a decade. (And not as a kicker or punter, either. A linebacker. He's not a small guy.) I have the appetite of a 350-pound wrestler, but it's rare that I actually give in and let my inner sumo eat whatever she wants. Here's one notable exception that sums up how ravenous I usually am: There is a restaurant in Manhattan called Eleven Madison Park, and it is justifiably famous for its exquisite food. It has a menu that changes with each season and that revolves entirely around the chef's selections. Each meal is at least eight courses long, and takes a minimum of three hours. It is nearly impossible to get a reservation, and yet for my birthday several years ago, my good friend Mary and I snagged a 5:30 table. We finished a little after 9:30. In those four hours, we had exquisite, painstakingly crafted morsels of food presented to us in ever more impressive fashion. A perfectly seared duo of clams on a small nest of sweet corn kernels was delivered under a little glass dome filled with briny smoke; once the dome was lifted, the ocean aroma conjured a New England clambake. Plate after plate came bearing three or four impeccable bites. Finally, Mary and I, who had entered the restaurant while the sun was still out, emerged into the night, still extolling the virtues of our nonstop eating experience. The presentation! The craftsmanship! The flavors!

That's when we decided to walk through Madison Square Park, the small leafy patch of green from which the restaurant, as well as the famed New York sports arena, takes its name. It is also home to the very first location of the Shake Shack, celebrated chef Danny Meyer's approach to fast food, serving insanely juicy burgers, milk shakes so thick they're called concretes, and fries so salty and golden they don't even need ketchup.

Mary and I began to walk across the park. We saw the Shake Shack. I stopped in my tracks and turned to her.

"Okay, you're going to totally think I'm crazy but..." I started.

"I will totally go and get a burger right now," Mary said, which is why I will love her forever and ever.

We had burgers and fries and concretes, and we finished every last bite. That night was probably one of the few times that I ate exactly what I wanted, and as much as I wanted. Here's a sentence I have never said: "I totally forgot to eat lunch today." Here's a sentence I say approximately five times a year: "I need to lose at least ten pounds." I am not, by any reasonable standard, overweight or unhealthy. I am, by insane Hollywood standards, which I encounter every time I step on a red carpet, approaching morbidly obese. I wish I could say that as I've grown older I've come to embrace a healthy and whole-minded approach to food that eschews fad diets and self-flagellation. The fact that I probably have three different fad diets in my browser history right now proves that's not true. It is true, however, that I've learned not to worry so much about being a size 8 in a world where 6 is the new 12 (that math simultaneously makes my head and soul hurt), and that I've accepted that there is no clothing size I have ever worn that is worth giving up carbs, the greatest food group on earth. That feels like progress to me.

Nevertheless, to say I've allowed food—how much I've eaten, what I'm going to eat, what I wished I hadn't eaten—to occupy a decent amount of my brain would be an understatement. So when it came to articles about "diet breakthroughs," which *Good Housekeeping* seemed to run every other month,

I was a fairly jaded soul. There was little that could be said on the matter that struck me as new, and *Good Housekeeping* didn't exactly try to break new ground in the diet and fitness world. Two magic words that would reliably sell covers for us, and which we would therefore use at least twice a year? *Belly Fat.* Hence the following cover lines: "Walk Off Belly Fat!" "Bye-Bye, Belly Fat!" "Banish Your Belly Fat!" When it came to weight-loss stories, we weren't in the habit of digging deep. I, personally, barely glanced at much of the diet content we printed, feeling both that I was too young for it to apply and that I had heard and seen it before anyway.

All of that changed after Wynonna Judd went on *Oprah*.

As a country musician, Wynonna had barely ever been on my radar when she was merely one half of the mother-daughter singing duo the Judds. Instead, what got my attention was the afternoon Wynonna sat down with Oprah Winfrey and said these words: "I have a problem with emotional eating."

It's a commonplace phrase now. But in 2004, the idea of someone identifying herself as an "emotional eater"—not simply someone lacking willpower or discipline but rather someone who ate to celebrate, to self-medicate, to soothe—was powerful. It was, as Oprah would say, an "Aha moment." Wynonna sat before Oprah and said she was on the verge of gastric bypass surgery but didn't want to go to that extreme. Instead, she wanted to get help, and she wanted to get to the root of what had led her to spend decades treating food as her drug of choice. Oprah, no stranger to that struggle, was all too happy to help, and promised to continue chronicling Wynonna's journey.

The day after Wynonna's episode aired, I practically ran

to Ellen's office. As I had felt about Kelly Ripa right after she was hired as Kathie Lee Gifford's replacement, I was now certain Wynonna was an exciting new cover option for *GH*, and was someone our readers would relate to and respect. We also needed a September cover.

"If I can get her to say everything to us that she said to Oprah, and talk all about how she's doing with her weight issues, will we give her the cover?" I breathlessly asked.

Ellen, to her credit, had by this point gotten fairly used to trusting my gut (no belly-related pun intended). One of the many things I adored about Ellen was that she was willing to admit that she might not be the authority on every single topic. She knew what she didn't know. And when it came to certain celebrities and their appeal, she was always willing to learn. She listened to what I had to say about Wynonna, as she had on Mariska and Kelly, and she gave me the go-ahead to pursue it.

After so often having to beg and cajole publicists to consider the cover of *GH*, it was always a thrill to approach a celebrity who needed no convincing. Wynonna was just that kind of star. The *GH* readership and the Oprah audience were essentially one and the same, and with an upcoming album and tour to promote, Wynonna's representatives were thrilled to be offered the September 2003 cover. Given the magazine's three-month lead time (meaning the amount of time in advance we needed to finish an issue before it would reach stands) this meant doing the interview and photo shoot in early June. As it turned out, Wynonna was going to be working on a project in Los Angeles, and suggested we do the interview at the Four Seasons Hotel in Beverly Hills, a location renowned for its discreet and exemplary service. I happily agreed.

I first met her at the photo shoot earlier that afternoon, where she shook my hand, then resumed chatting happily with the hairstylist about her greatest hits. When the stylist mentioned that his mother was a huge fan, Wynonna didn't hesitate.

"Well, let's call her, honey," she said, and a few minutes later, she was crooning one of her songs into the phone while the stylist's mom sobbed on the other end. Wynonna went on to pose in various outfits during the shoot, over several hours. By the time we were done, she was clearly exhausted. I worried for a moment that she might try to postpone the interview, and I had a flight back to New York the next morning. But she came over to me and told me she'd meet me at the hotel in thirty minutes.

I got there before her, and noticed that when she pulled up in the SUV being driven by her then-husband, she sat in the front seat and hung her head for a moment before getting out, seemingly trying to muster some energy. Something in her seemed a little beaten down and weary, but I chalked it up to the photo shoot's having taken its toll. She sat down across from me and we ordered a large plate of veggies with some low-fat dip (this being Los Angeles, of course such options were on the menu) and began to talk about her battle to conquer her issues with diet and exercise, which at this point she was waging with the aid of Oprah's personal trainer, Bob Greene. Wynonna didn't hide the fact that she often felt discouraged.

"I'm doing all this work and then it's like, 'Congratulations!

You lost one inch from your neck!'" she said with a small sneer.

Already, she was bristling against public expectations of how much she was planning to lose.

"People ask me about my goal weight," she said with a sigh. "I just say, 'Well, I'm trying to get back to my original weight…eight pounds, fifteen ounces, here I come!"

She recalled an early memory of eating cereal late at night with her grandmother, and the feeling of comfort she got— both from the cereal and from being with a family member who loved her so unconditionally. Wynonna's relationship with her own mom, Naomi, was famously rocky, and so it wasn't hard to understand how the soothing presence of Wynonna's grandmother and the filling effect of some corn-flakes could become powerfully intertwined.

She gave me plenty of great quotes about emotional eating; Bob Greene also provided a motivational sidebar that we included in the story. But I left the Four Seasons knowing that we wouldn't have an incredible "reveal" cover the following year where we could show Wynonna, having lost a hundred pounds, suddenly showing off her svelte new figure. Wynonna knew it, too, and at one point said to me, "I'm not gonna go on *Oprah* in a bikini."

As it turns out, a year later, she did something much better.

The Wynonna cover in September 2003 sold so well that the following year we decided to put her on the cover again, for the September 2004 issue. It didn't matter that she hadn't lost much weight; clearly, readers liked Wynonna just as she was. I would once again return for the photo shoot and inter-view, but this time, both would happen on the same day, just outside Nashville in Franklin, Tennessee, where Wynonna lived.

Weeks later, I arrived in Nashville and checked into the strangest hotel I've ever stayed in: the Gaylord Opryland, a sort of cross between a hotel and an indoor shopping mall, in which rooms faced an internal courtyard filled with restaurants like Chick-fil-A and shops selling Grand Ole Opry souvenirs. The following afternoon, after far too much of the aforementioned Chick-fil-A, I headed to the photo studio, which was in a completely nondescript and suburban part of town and where our photographer George Holz had been setting up since that morning.

When I walked in, I immediately began scouting for a quiet area where I could interview Wynonna later that afternoon. No mention had been made of another location for us to talk, so I assumed we'd be chatting at the studio. George had a variety of couches and chairs he was moving on and off the set, and I figured any of them would suffice. Then I saw Wynonna. Or, more accurately, she spotted me.

Her hair, orange with streaks of Crayola red, was set in huge foam rollers, and she was wearing a bowling shirt festooned with drawings of Elvis. She walked over to me, her flip-flops slapping against the concrete floor.

"Hi Wynonna..." I started, extending my hand.

"Oh honey, this is the South. We hug here," she cut me off, pulling me into an embrace.

A few moments later, the wardrobe stylist came over to us. "Wynonna, you need to start trying on a few different looks," she said. Photo shoots don't involve outfits but rather "looks"—complete ensembles that are supposed to set the tone for the entire magazine. In the spring, the look should be clean, light, pretty. In the winter, the look is deeper, richer, cozier. For Wynonna, and considering the color of her hair, everything she tried on was in a jewel-toned autumnal palate. Wynonna looked at the rack of clothing waiting for her and sighed.

"I'd honestly rather go to the gynecologist," she groaned, then reluctantly flip-flopped over to the changing area.

For the next several hours, Wynonna gamely posed in a variety of looks and positions. She posed with her guitar. She straddled a chair. She lounged on a couch. She threw her head back and laughed on command even though no one had said anything funny. If you think you don't mind having your photo taken, I suggest trying to do it for roughly five hours straight. It is exhausting, awkward, and completely draining. Doing it when you don't exactly love the shape you're in makes it exponentially harder. I tried to slip in a few interview questions with Wynonna whenever she had her hair touched up or during a quick lunch break, but it was clear I was going to have to wait until the shoot was over to get the bulk of the story done, and I was worried that once again she'd seem drained and beleaguered after hours spent contorting herself and sweating under the studio lights.

Finally, after cheerfully posing for a photo with George, and another one with our art director, and finally one with me, Wynonna was finished. As the crew began to pack away props, I started to fix up the best corner of the cavernous studio where we could sit and talk. I had pushed two armchairs together in close proximity and went to get Wynonna when I saw she was already standing by the door of the studio with her car keys in her hand.

"You ready to get out of here?" she said to me, smiling and full of energy. I had no idea where we were supposed to be going.

"Sure!" I said, hoping I sounded confident as opposed to clueless.

"You need a ride or you want to follow me?" she asked.

As it turned out, I had taken a cab to the studio and so I did need a ride. Which is how I wound up in Wynonna Judd's Range Rover—emblazoned with a large bumper sticker reading MY BOSS IS A JEWISH CARPENTER—as she drove us to an old-school Southern cooking legend called Dotson's.

Family-owned for nearly fifty years at that point, Dotson's had a wraparound front porch that evoked cowboys tying up their horses before heading in for whiskey. Instead, an impressive number of Ford F-150s filled the lot. Inside, the walls were lined with knotty-pine paneling, tables were topped with Formica, and the booths were a deep red vinyl. It was clear from the warm greeting Wynonna received as we walked in that she was a regular. It became even clearer when I noticed that several of the white photocopied menus slid into vinyl holders bore her autograph on the front.

Sliding into opposite sides of the booth, Wynonna and I were handed menus by a waitress who called us both Hon and then quickly went to get us some water. I scanned the menu and quickly grew concerned. Raw veggies and low-fat dip were not going to be an option at Dotson's. Not that I particularly minded: if you go back several generations in my family, you hit a whole wave of ancestors who came from Alabama. Their genes are alive and well in me, and I would have liked nothing more than to have a metabolism that would have allowed me to eat every single thing I saw listed at Dotson's: fried chicken, barbecued brisket, macaroni and cheese, pinto beans, collard greens, biscuits, cornbread. It was everything I'd ever wanted to eat, all in one place. Yet here I was with Wynonna Judd, a woman who, when I had last checked, was in the depths of her struggle against emotional eating. Here...in what seemed to be a shrine to the Almighty Butter.

The waitress reappeared, and I noticed—as I had before she ran off to get water—that she seemed to be anxiously hopping from foot to foot. Wynonna finally glanced away from the menu and up at her.

"Well, how are you doin', Sweetheart?" she drawled.

It was all the encouragement the waitress needed.

"Oh, I just love you," she said, in a way that sounded only half as creepy as it did when I occasionally blurted it out to famous people. Maybe it was the Deep South accent that helped her pull it off in a way I could not.

"And you know, I don't even like country music," the waitress continued. "But I love you. You're really the best. I love your hair. And your shirt!" She pointed at the Elvis shirt Wynonna was once again wearing.

For the next five minutes, the waitress proceeded to tell us her life story—everything from how long she'd been working at Dotson's to the failure of her first two marriages. I completely forgot to be nervous about what I would order in front of Wynonna and instead marveled at the server's ability to ceaselessly unburden herself to us, two total strangers. Finally, Wynonna cut her off, though not unkindly.

"Darlin', I think we can order," she said, then looked over at me. "I've had everything here. Unless there's something you know you'll hate, you mind if I just get all the best stuff they have?"

I had no objection. And with that, Wynonna ordered fried chicken, fried okra, collard greens, macaroni and cheese, mashed potatoes, sweet potatoes, and cornbread. Then she uttered one of the most beautiful sentences I've ever heard another person say:

"You still got a piece of that chocolate cola cake left back there? Save us some of that," Wynonna told the waitress.

I honestly don't know if I've ever been happier.

The waitress wrote it all down, then gazed at Wynonna again.

"Oh, I wish you'd just take me home with you," she half-gasped, before looking worriedly over her shoulder. "I'm sorry. I should shut up. The manager says I talk too much, but if you see him, you'll tell him I was okay, won't you?" she asked.

"Of course I will, Honey," Wynonna said.

The waitress hurried off and Wynonna looked to me and raised one expertly groomed eyebrow.

"I used to be like that," she said. "Before I got on medication."

I had expected Wynonna to be more at ease than last time, if only because we were in her hometown and it was our second interview together. Still, the extent to which she was warm, wise, and witty was a happy surprise. She spoke openly about her issues with food, and acknowledged that perhaps her dinner order seemed a little unexpected, particularly in front of a reporter. She was wholly unapologetic about it.

"People who say you have to deprive yourself of carbs or whatever can kiss my big butt," she said. "Because this is what happens: you deprive yourself of what you love until you crave it so badly that you binge on it. Now I'm at a point where I satisfy my cravings, but I don't go overboard," she said. I quickly realized that she was going to be radically different than anyone I had ever interviewed before—including the Wynonna I'd interviewed twelve months earlier. Certainly, she was less filtered and far more candid. When I asked her about a specific goal weight, she just shrugged, and then offered some advice to *GH* readers.

"Ladies, throw out your scales!" she half-shouted into my tape recorder. "Weighing yourself every morning is as pointless as a man measuring his penis every morning. Don't do it!"

The food arrived, and the waitress seemed as if she might indeed have been reprimanded by the owner by that point, because she delivered plate after plate of home-cooked goodness in virtual silence. I hardly knew where to start—the fried chicken? the collard greens?—but I picked up my fork as I continued to deliberate.

"Oh no," Wynonna exclaimed, and I suddenly thought something might have been wrong with the food. *Have they forgotten the biscuits? The mac and cheese? Not the mac and cheese!* I looked up and saw her extending both hands across the table to me.

"We need to give thanks," she said pointedly.

It is officially the only time I have ever prayed with a celebrity. We clasped hands across the table and bowed our heads. I closed my eyes for a minute then opened them to sneak a peek at Wynonna, who had both of her eyes closed. For a split second I panicked that she might expect me to say something, but I needn't have worried. Wynonna began to thank the Lord for not only the bounty of food before us but for several other blessings—friends, family, and everyone's continued health—before finally giving my hands a squeeze and saying, "Thank you for the opportunity to sit and learn," then adding an "Amen."

I repeated her "Amen" and then watched to see if it was okay to pick up my fork. When I saw her dig in, I knew I was free to do the same.

As we continued to talk in between bites of the flaky biscuits and sweet cornbread (me, carb-loading as if I were running a marathon the next day) and collard greens and chicken (her, sticking to what were arguably the healthiest choices on the table), it became clear that the Jewish Carpenter bumper sticker wasn't the only motto of which Wynonna was fond. Speaking in aphorisms was something of a strong suit for her.

"So, how did you feel when Oprah said you needed to change your diet and..." I began.

"It's not a diet. It's a live-it," Wynonna interjected. She went on to say that she'd discovered that her emotional eating was but a major symptom of her lifelong desire to please everyone else, while putting her own needs last. Food became her closest friend. Now, she said, she was learning new coping mechanisms, which included making her own needs a priority. As it turned out, sometimes what she needed was to simply not care so much about what other people thought of her.

"This isn't about entertainment; this is my real life," she said of no longer worrying about being an Oprah-worthy success story. "I'm not going to worry about how many pounds I've lost; I'm just going to try not to do the things that were destructive."

I asked how her relationship with her mother, Naomi, still somewhat fraught, had changed in light of all the self-discovery she'd been doing. She explained she was now in a state of what she termed "radical forgiveness."

"I'm learning to communicate with her in a way that doesn't break her spirit because I want to honor what's honorable about her," she said. "But I'm not going to obey her for the rest of my life, you know?"

"But still, when you're confronted with a real conflict with her, given the stress that must bring up, how do you handle that sort of dilemma…" I started to say. But Wynonna was ready with another winner.

"Honey," she said, holding up a hand to stop me from talking. "When life gives you a dilemma, you make di-lemonade."

If I'm ever inspired to get a lengthy and ill-advised tattoo, I'm going to make it that sentence right there.

In that little restaurant that day, Wynonna spoke more openly than any A-list celebrity I've ever interviewed. No topic—her children, her marriage, her finances, her mother—was off-limits. An hour, then another one, flew by. Eventually, I looked at the table in front of me and realized I had emptied nearly all of my dishes. And meanwhile, Wynonna was right: barely half of her food was touched.

"Hon, we're about done here," she called to the waitress, who came to clear everything away.

What about the cake? I wanted to ask. But of course cake wasn't important, I scolded myself inwardly. Meanwhile, another little voice replied, *"Cake cake cake it's chocolate coca cola cake. Caaaaake."* As the cake battle raged on in my head, Wynonna imparted some more wisdom.

"Instead of beating myself up for the ten things I didn't do,

I'm going to appreciate the two things I did do," she said. "I'm going to start celebrating myself."

You know what's a good way to celebrate? With cake, I wanted to say, but I managed to control myself.

Then Wynonna looked at me and raised an eyebrow again. "You ready for some cake?" she asked. I'm still amazed that I didn't reach across the table and kiss her.

The cake was sublime: you don't taste the cola at all, just the sweet tanginess it leaves behind. Wynonna went to use the ladies room and while she was gone I signaled for the check. This time the owner, not the waitress, came over.

"Your money's no good here. She eats on the house," she explained. I tried to insist, explaining that it wasn't my money, really, but a business expense.

"No, Ma'am," the owner replied. "Any friend of hers, even a new one, is a friend of ours. She's the greatest, isn't she?"

It wasn't hard for me to agree.

In the ensuing years since that interview, Wynonna's weight has remained essentially constant, despite a brief stint as a spokesperson for a weight-loss drug. She's never going to be a thin girl; neither am I. But she's one of the first people who showed me—and twenty-six million *Good Housekeeping* readers—that maybe I don't have to beat myself up over it. That maybe the best version of who you are is the version you are right now.

Only one thing has truly changed. Just last year, Dotson's closed after sixty years. If anyone has the recipe for their chocolate cola cake, please find a way to get it to me. As I'm sure Wynonna herself would say if only she'd thought of it, "The only way to have your cake and eat it too…is to order two slices."

Six Things Never to Order When
Dining with a Celebrity

If I'm sitting across a restaurant table from a gorgeous, talented, and much-loved human, it is likely because I'm on the job (no offense to my husband). That means I have work to do, and can't be worried about making a terrible impression based on what I'm eating. Next time you're dining with a star, remember to skip the following:

1. **Oil-and-vinegar-based dressing.** You will be tempted, sure, to get the ubiquitous "balsamic vinaigrette." If you do, beware and proceed with caution. Tiny, oil-rimmed little brown flecks of dressing have been known to leap right off lettuce leaves and on to silk blouses without warning, an issue that doesn't exist with heavier, creamier dressings. Get the ranch, and get it on the side.

2. **Chicken nuggets.** Even if they are called something fancy like "panko-breaded chicken fingerlings" they are still chicken nuggets, and you shouldn't order them in front of someone you are trying to impress, unless you are both under the age of ten.

3. **Anything red.** Tomato sauce is not your friend, and it will inevitably wind up somewhere on your body where you do not want it. Ditto barbeque sauce, or any sort of vegetable-broth-based soup. See above re: stained clothing.

4. **Spaghetti, regardless of topping**. Even if you avoid the dreaded red sauce, no one needs to see you twirling and slurping, especially not a multimillionaire movie star. Also, carbs in Hollywood? Ew.

5. **Onions or garlic**. Odds are high that you will not get close enough to a star for them to smell your breath. But there is absolutely no reason to risk it, because the one time you opt for the garlicky Caesar salad will wind up being the one time you suddenly need to help a celebrity adjust her contact lens and get right into her face in order to do so.

6. **Alcohol**. Never, ever. If the star sitting across from you orders a glass of wine, rejoice inwardly because a great interview may soon follow. But do not follow suit. If you feel pressured into doing so, order one glass of wine and take tiny sips that never let the contents get below the halfway mark. In other words: nurse that one glass all night—and pray your companion gets lots and lots of refills.

Chapter 5

Tom Cruise Is Going to Marry Me Someday

AFTER A FEW YEARS AT *GOOD HOUSEKEEPING*, OBTAIN-ing big names for the cover had gotten marginally easier. Ellen was comfortable with taking calculated risks, and I had started to perfect the art of begging for the right mega-star at the right time. On my watch, we had featured everyone from Paula Deen (a risk, which paid off big time) to Sandra Bullock (mega-star, promoting *Hope Floats*, in which she played a mom). But there was one category of star that permanently represented a rarity among *GH* covers: men. We almost never featured a man on the cover, unless that man was such an indisputable sex symbol that his face would inspire enough women to swoon their way to the checkout stand. As it turned out, in the spring of 2006, I would wind up dealing with two such men, within forty-eight hours.

By that April, two celebrity actors were making headlines. The first was Patrick Dempsey. Amazingly, the geek from *Can't Buy Me Love* had become the biggest heartthrob on the planet, thanks to his role as Dr. Derek "McDreamy" Shepherd on *Grey's Anatomy*. Patrick had been simmering for a few years before that, with a plot arc on *Will & Grace* and a role as a total babe in *Sweet Home Alabama*. Now he was having the sort of career resurgence that any star would envy, slowly segueing from near-obscurity into a completely different spotlight—as a hunky leading man with matinee idol good looks that made women everywhere swoon. I was already bracing myself to be one of those women. While he'd done *GQ* and other men's magazines, his publicity team wanted him to do a cover that represented his level of mainstream success. It was hard to get more mainstream than *Good Housekeeping*. With a movie, *Enchanted* (costarring an up-and-coming actress named Amy Adams), coming out later in the year, I pushed for Patrick to appear on an upcoming cover. I was thrilled when Ellen and, most importantly, Patrick's publicists, agreed. A date was set for an interview in Los Angeles, followed by a photo shoot in New York City when Patrick was in town a few weeks later.

Meanwhile, on a completely different section of the A-list, Tom Cruise was continuing to weather a maelstrom of controversy. While doing publicity for his film *War of the Worlds* one year earlier, he had decided to become more outspoken about his involvement in Scientology and about his love for the actress Katie Holmes. Everyone remembers what happened next: jumping on couches on *Oprah*, calling Matt Lauer "glib." Most notable to the staff at *Good Housekeeping* was the moment when he expressed concern that Brooke

Shields had used antidepressants to help recover from the postpartum depression she had suffered after the birth of her daughter Rowan. "When someone says (medication) has helped them, it is to cope, it didn't cure anything. There is no science," Tom had said, going on to add that he felt vitamins and exercise were a better option for postpartum sufferers.

His words particularly raised eyebrows at the *GH* offices because we had featured Brooke on our cover and had done the exclusive excerpt from her book, *Down Came the Rain*, when she first discussed her postpartum depression. I had personally selected the excerpt from the book, and had been the one to interview Brooke. As I had hoped and expected, Brooke was smart and funny (and astonishingly beautiful) and also very direct and open about how she had suffered. It was clear just to look at her—though still weary from life with a toddler at that point—that she felt tremendously relieved to have made it through such a terribly dark time.

Now Tom Cruise was once again going to have to face the press, less than ten months after his last round of talk shows and magazines, this time to promote *Mission: Impossible III*. Many in the media, myself included, expected this to be Tom Cruise: The Apology Tour. His publicity team surely must have felt that there could be no more incidents like the one with Brooke or Matt Lauer.

As I had with Jennifer Lopez, I hoped I might be able to sell his publicists on the power of *Good Housekeeping* to present a kinder, gentler version of their star. I figured his team would be looking for a safe harbor, and I quickly called to offer one. By that point, Tom—who was now expecting a child with his fiancée, Katie—was showing a far more congenial side of himself than he had during *War of the Worlds* publicity, and I was adamant that he show that side to *GH*'s readers. "We won't let him look crazy!" I insisted to the studio publicist for the film. My pleas worked, and we finally settled on an interview date, also in Los Angeles...in fact, one day before I was scheduled to meet with Patrick Dempsey. I don't know when I've ever been happier to book a cross-country economy-class flight.

The night I arrived in LA, I talked to my best friend, Stephanie, about how excited I was for both interviews. I was particularly looking forward to meeting Patrick, whose incredible blue eyes alone could launch a thousand fantasies. Admittedly, I had never really had much of a crush on Tom Cruise as a teen; I'll confess that in *Top Gun*, I was more attracted to Val Kilmer's Iceman than Tom's Maverick. (Don't judge until you've seen *Real Genius*.) Then there was the fact that the Scientology jokes came almost too easily.

"Don't let him talk you into joining the Sea-Org!" Stephanie said, only half-kiddingly, about one faction of Scientology. "Don't fall for any brainwashing tactics!"

I agreed and, privately, found myself feeling like the Cruise interview was the daunting hurdle I had to get over before I could reach the Promised Land that was breakfast with Patrick.

———

The next morning, I went to meet Tom at Le Parker Meridien, a high-end yet not super-elite hotel in Hollywood. It was an odd choice, as stars tend to flock to one of two establishments in Los Angeles when it comes time to meet the press. There's the ultra-luxurious Four Seasons in Beverly Hills, where I'd first interviewed Wynonna Judd, where Angelina Jolie holed up with her newly adopted son Maddox as her marriage to Billy Bob Thornton fell apart, and where nearly every celebrity likes to stay during awards season—even those with homes only a dozen miles away. The Four Seasons is the kind of hotel where the scent of some unidentifiable but exceedingly rare orchid scents the perfectly climate-controlled air. It is the kind of hotel where iced tea comes with ice cubes made out of…iced tea. (I'll give you a minute to ponder the genius of that.) On the other end of the luxury spectrum is the Chateau Marmont, the hotel that was made for hipsters before hipsters even existed. It's known as the hotel where John Belushi died, where Lindsay Lohan liked to drink, and where the air is scented with some unidentifiable blend of tobacco, whiskey, and musk. It is also, in a way that the Four Seasons would never even try to be, deeply cool. In fact, the Chateau (as it is always called) was the very place where I was going to have breakfast with Patrick Dempsey. That made perfect sense. But I couldn't understand why I was meeting Tom Cruise at Le Parker Meridien, a hotel that is not known for anything or anyone, and which smells vaguely like industrial carpeting.

When I walked into the hotel, the doorman greeted me by saying, "Welcome to the Le Meridien," a phrasing which made me stop despite having nearly failed high school French. At the front desk, the gentleman who gave me the room number similarly welcomed me to "the Le Meridien." Is there anyone who doesn't know "Le" means "the"? Apparently, at least two staffers at the Le Meridien do not.

I was shown to a large but fairly nondescript suite that had enough food in it to feed a football team. A huge spread contained fruit, cold cuts, cheese, and crackers, and another platter was overflowing with brownies and cookies. There were five different kinds of sodas, and different juices and bottled waters. It was more food than we at *GH* normally brought in for a full-day photo shoot, and this was just a ninety-minute interview.

I'm not sure if I can adequately describe what it is like to sit and wait for Tom Cruise to walk into a room. It's sort of like waiting for a blind date, job interview, and first meeting with your future in-laws all wrapped into one. I was too nervous to eat anything as I paced around the empty room. I noticed a tape recorder on a table in the living room area, and wondered what it was for; I had brought my own as always. I checked my hair seventeen times, and my teeth for lipstick. I contemplated using the bathroom but became terrified that Tom would walk in just as I was flushing. Finally, feeling like a fool for pacing around like a caged tiger, I forced myself to sit on the couch.

Two minutes later, the door swung open and Tom walked in, wearing jeans, dark boots, and a thin black cashmere sweater. I had prepared myself for him to be short, as the press makes a big deal out of how diminutive he is, but he was taller than I am by a couple of inches, and seemed to be comprised entirely out of charisma, teeth, and glistening chestnut hair to rival an Irish setter.

"Hey there, Kate, it's great to meet you," he said, making direct eye contact and shaking my hand firmly.

"Hi!" I said. "Welcome to the Le Meridien!"

I inhaled deeply as I realized what I'd said, and prayed he wouldn't think I was an idiot.

"Wait…" he said hesitantly. "Did you just say 'the Le Meridien'?"

"Yes!" I exclaimed. "It's what they say downstairs! I swear! They say 'the Le Meridien!'"

"Oh no," Tom laughed. "That's ridiculous. I wonder if they serve their roast beef 'with *au jus* sauce'?"

I let out a happy and relieved sigh. So far so good.

I walked over to the living room area of the suite and motioned to the couch where I had been sitting, then headed toward a chair across from him. I also noticed that his publicist, who had trailed him into the room, had quietly turned on the tape recorder I'd spotted before and had then slipped back out again. (To this day, he is the only celebrity to have also recorded an interview that I was recording. When I think about how much sense it makes for a celebrity, particularly one known for having to handle controversy, to have proof of what they said, I'm surprised more subjects don't do this.) As I began to take my seat opposite him, Tom stopped me.

"No, don't sit all the way over there. That's too far away. Sit here," he said, patting the couch next to him.

I calmly walked to the couch, while inside my head a voice screamed, *"Tom Cruise wants you to sit next to him! You could totally touch Tom Cruise right now if you wanted to!"* I'm not sure why my inner super-fan consistently goes bonkers at the reality of being able to touch a famous person, but inevitably, that is the fact that always blows my mind: this person, this star I've seen on screens a million times, is now so close that if I wanted to poke him in the ribs, or run my fingers through his hair, I could. Mayhem and possibly legal proceedings would ensue, but technically, I could.

As I sat down, I asked him all the usual warm-up questions: how his press tour had been going so far, what his plans were for the coming weeks, if he was going to get a break from promoting at any point. Tom maintained eye contact throughout, frequently using my name, and often reaching out and touching my forearm to make a point. Honestly? It quickly became a little hard not to feel a mild buzz from his intensity and energy. Renée Zellweger, after making *Jerry Maguire* with him, later said, "You'd look into his eyes and he'd really be there, he'd really be in love with you. You could see his heart and soul. And then the director would shout 'Cut,' Tom would leave the set, and you'd have to go into therapy for six months." I was beginning to understand how she felt.

He effortlessly and eagerly told stories about his children, Bella and Connor, with his ex-wife, Nicole Kidman, and spoke movingly about how he made no distinction between the biological child Katie was now carrying and his two kids who had been adopted.

"No way. There's no difference. I'm the one who changed their diapers, who stayed up with them at night. You cannot separate that bond... People used to come up to me and say, 'Are you going to have your own children?'" he recalled, aghast. "And I'd just say, 'What do you mean? I do have my own. They are my own.'" At times, his voice became choked with emotion. At others, he would laugh so uproariously and with such intensity his eyes would seem to well up. It was a pretty heady scent he was giving off.

I eventually started to move the discussion toward his comments about Brooke, to whom he had already personally made amends some months earlier; she had since publicly accepted what she said was a "heartfelt" apology. (Just this past year, *People* did a story with Brooke in which she mentioned their reconciliation and how she took him to task: "I said, 'Come on, you don't even have ovaries. Why are you fighting this?' He said, 'I know, Brooke, I know.' He laughed. He's got humor, too.") While I understood the Brooke fight was water under the bridge, I still asked pointedly about his feelings on antidepressants. This was where I expected some similar groveling to commence. But Tom surprised me by not backing down.

"Look, I know this is controversial," he said, pointing out that the FDA now required "black box" warnings—which indicate a drug may carry a significant risk of serious side effects—on all antidepressant medications, alerting consumers to an increased risk of suicidal tendencies in children and adolescents. "And people don't have to listen to me," he continued. "But people should find out about this for themselves. I really do care about people, and I care about the way that their lives are being harmed by these drugs. Don't get me wrong: I believe in proper medical care. If you have cancer, you need medicine. And I'm not saying that women, men, and children don't come up against problems in life. But drugs aren't the solution...Now there's this huge industry, this machine, pushing us to hurry up and put our kids on drugs. Well, you know what I say to that machine? I say screw you."

As a person with loved ones who have been profoundly helped by antidepressants, I didn't agree with his position against them, or against psychiatry for that matter. I nevertheless had to respect the fact that Tom was sticking to his convictions, and not changing what he believed for the sake of more favorable spin or better media coverage. As he talked about the surprisingly old-fashioned way he was raising his children—"You want a clean room? Then you have to clean your room. No one is going to do it for you," he explained—I off-handedly mentioned that my husband was a schoolteacher.

"He is?" Tom said, genuinely interested. "That's fantastic. How long have you been together?"

I replied that by that point we'd known each other for over a decade.

"Do you guys have kids?" Tom asked, before adding, "No, wait: Back up. How did you two meet?"

I spared him by giving him the shortest version of the story that I possibly could: my husband and I met as camp counselors when he was nineteen and I was eighteen. He was the hunky football player who would never have noticed me in high school—I tutored guys like him, I didn't date them. But free from high school labels, we dated for two years. Then, thanks to attending colleges that were thousands of miles and one whole continent apart (while I was at Oxford, he was at college in upstate New York), we broke up, painfully, and each of us moved on to other relationships that ultimately proved disastrous. And then, nearly ten years later, he saw me plugging a *GH* story on *Entertainment Tonight*. (This was before Facebook or social media would have made getting back in touch far easier and more probable.) The next day, my phone rang at the office, and it was him. Two days later, we had dinner. Ten months later, he drove me back up to the camp where we'd first met and proposed. Eventually, we got married. No kids yet, I explained to Tom, but time would tell. The end.

My actual retelling contained far more detail than the brief summary I just gave; my husband teases me that when we're at a party and someone asks me how we met, he knows he has plenty of time to go to the bar, get another drink and probably a few rounds of hors d'oeuvres before he has to return to my side. But as I tried to truncate my epic tale, Tom kept laughing or asking follow-up questions or nodding his head vigorously. Not even my shrink had ever been so actively engaged in what I had to say, and I paid that guy a small fortune. By the time I finished my story, Tom looked at me with his mouth slightly open.

"That is so incredible. You have to write about that someday. That's a true love story right there," he said. "Promise me you'll write about that."

"Okay, I'll get right on that, I promise," I said with a hint of sarcasm, before offering a smooth segue: "Now, tell me about your great love story."

He began to talk about Katie Holmes—or Kate, as he called her—in a tone that could only be described as rapturous. He sounded the way I do when I talk about macaroni and cheese. He talked about watching movies at home with her, playing board games, doing simple things you would imagine any normal couple doing.

"She's the love of my life," he said simply. "I knew I was done the minute I met her."

Always a wise-ass, I motioned to the couch we were sitting on. "Hey, feel free to jump on the couch if you need to," I offered. I was hoping that by then, after an hour of trading life stories, we were comfortable enough with each other that he could handle a little good-natured ribbing.

Tom looked at me and smiled, and cocked one eyebrow. And then he slowly, deliberately, stepped up onto the couch and began to jump. His cashmere sweater rose with each bounce and I could see an exposed sliver of ripped abdominal muscle and a thin line of hair. At this point the little voice in my head had a total nervous breakdown: *"You can see Tom Cruise's stomach! You could totally touch his bare flesh!"* I stopped just short of having a full-blown Hannibal-Lecter-nice-Chianti moment in which I deeply sucked in the air around him through my mouth.

He sat back down, and looked at me.

"I know that I'm with the woman I want to spend the rest of my life with," he said, touching my forearm again, and fixing me with his hazel-eyed gaze. In that moment it became clear to me that, despite his adoration for Katie, he was also in love with *me*. I mean—the constant use of my name, the unwavering eye contact, the not-at-all-feigned interest in everything I had to say: it was all so obvious. Yes, we were both otherwise committed. But for a fleeting second, my inner schoolgirl ripped down my Val Kilmer poster and practiced writing "Mrs. Tom Cruise" a few dozen times in a spiral notebook.

At that very moment, the door to the suite swung open and in walked a very pregnant, very beautiful Katie Holmes. A few of the tabloids had been speculating at that point that the pregnancy was a hoax and that she was actually just wearing pregnancy padding to conceal the fact that Scientology was buying them a baby from somewhere. Yes, someone actually printed that. Even worse, enough people actually read it that when I later mentioned I had met Katie, a few of them seriously asked, "Is she really pregnant?" I saw the woman's ankles: Trust me, she was pregnant.

Now, I'm not sure how most people in the world say hello to their significant others. My opening comments to my husband fall on a spectrum that ranges anywhere from "Hi honey" to "Where the hell have you been?" I can safely say I have never, ever, greeted anyone the way Tom Cruise and Katie Holmes greeted each other.

"I love you," he said upon seeing her, then getting up and crossing the room toward her.

"I love you," she replied, looking at him in a way that felt like it should have been accompanied by twinkling little cartoon stars in her eyes.

When I wrote about the moment for *Good Housekeeping*, I said they were like two kids on Christmas morning who had just unwrapped exactly what they wanted. I still can't think of a better description for the sheer giddiness they seemed to have around each other. They were besotted. If it was an act, they both deserved Oscars. Tom introduced us, and I lamely offered that I, too, was once a Katie who now preferred Kate. She smiled sweetly.

"Oh, wait!" Tom said suddenly to me. "I want you to hear the song."

Kanye West had recorded a version of the *Mission: Impossible* theme song for the new film. Early in our conversation,

Tom had mentioned he wanted me to hear it, adding, "But we need to get a boom box in here or something that can play a CD."

Now, miraculously, a small stereo with a CD player had appeared. Because, when you're Tom Cruise and you say that you need a stereo, stealth ninjas creep into the room and supply one or something. Tom pulled the CD out of an envelope sitting on a table and slid it in, then turned the volume up as far as it would go. Soon, a pulsing rhythmic beat began to blare out of the stereo, while Tom and Katie grinned wildly. Then Tom started to dance.

I have read countless articles in the ensuing years about the remarkable feats Tom Cruise has accomplished: even after turning fifty he insisted on doing many of his own stunts. He can rock climb, parachute, kickbox, fly a plane, drive a race-car, and sing several octaves above a high C. But I have yet to see his dance moves properly detailed in any of the extensive discussions of him. Allow me to do the honors.

To describe Tom's dance style as the white man's overbite (bite your bottom lip while pumping fists lamely) doesn't really do it justice. There is an additional move—something akin to pantomiming driving a car, whereby you must squat slightly while putting one arm straight out and moving it from side to side—that puts the Tom Cruise Dance truly over the edge. I was both stunned and thrilled: the journalist in me knew it would make for a great detail in the story (and it did). The super-fan in me knew I would now get to tell my friends I'd gotten along so well with Tom Cruise that he'd danced for me (and I did). As my Southern grandmother would say: Bless his heart. Tom loved the song, and he couldn't help but dance along to it any more than he could help jumping on the couch. Heavily pregnant Katie, poor thing, could merely sway back and forth. I, meanwhile, looked around nervously. Was I supposed to dance? Was Tom expecting me to join in this party somehow? I didn't want to. I wouldn't. I couldn't.

In the years that have followed, I have always told people I refused to dance, and just good-naturedly bobbed my head along to the song. That's a lie. Of course I danced. When Tom Cruise starts dancing in front of you, you dance right along with him. I don't know what you would call my moves. The Regrettably Awkward Girl? The Are You Okay? There were no little kicks or hooked thumbs involved, but I'm sure I was barely much better than Elaine Benes. (If you're not a *Seinfeld* fan, go Google "Elaine Benes Seinfeld Dance." I'll wait here.) Mostly, I've blocked out what I must have done, though I like to tell myself I refrained from clapping or snapping at any point. I'm sure it was all the smoothness of myself at a junior high mixer combined with the added self-consciousness of standing in front of two of the biggest stars in the world. I'm also sure it wasn't pretty. As the song continued, I found myself wondering how long Kanye West could possibly rap about the impossible missions, and prayed it wasn't as long as he could rap about his own greatness. Mercifully, the song was only about three minutes long, and it was over soon. (A few years later, Tom, in a fat suit and heavy makeup, would of course show astonishing agility and footwork as sleazy agent Les Grossman in *Tropic Thunder*, proving that when Tom Cruise really wants to bust a move, he can.)

When the music finally stopped, I heaved a sigh of relief— which Tom and Katie took to mean I was blown away by the music. "He's unbelievably talented, right?" Tom asked, and I agreed immediately, though secretly I feared he might ask me if I wanted to listen to the song again. Instead, Tom's publicist reappeared, and Tom and Katie said their goodbyes. Then they were gone, exiting through the back of the hotel via the kitchen. I know because when I waited for my car from the valet in the front of the hotel, I lamely scanned the street for them, hoping I would spot them so they could approach me and say, "Hey! There you are! We forgot to invite you to dinner!"

That didn't happen. Instead, Tom's publicist caught up with me as I waited for my car.

"I think Tom really enjoyed his time with you," he said. "And actually, he was wondering what your plans for tomorrow were..."

I felt my knees almost buckle. Here it was! An invitation to the Cruise-Holmes house! I was going to be invited into their inner sanctum!

I was right...almost. I just had the wrong inner sanctum.

"Because we'd be happy to arrange for a tour of the Scientology Center for you," the publicist was continuing to say. "It takes a few hours, but you might find it very worthwhile."

I swallowed my disappointment and smiled. No matter how much I adored the man, I had my limits. I politely declined the invitation and drove back to my hotel.

Once in my room, I called Stephanie, where I calmly and objectively told her about my time with Tom.

"Oh my god," I said the minute she picked up. "I absolutely loved him. He is just so fantastic. And he loved me, too!"

"Oh shit," Stephanie said. "You're a Scientologist now, aren't you? I cannot believe how easy you are. You just fall in love with anyone, don't you? You know there's a name for people like you. It starts with 'Star' and ends with a word that rhymes with 'Trucker.'"

"Shut up," I told her. "I am not one of those. You know how much I hated that bitch from that cable show I interviewed last week. I don't just love anyone."

Later that night, however, I found myself worried that Stephanie had a point. Sure, I had turned down the Scientology tour invite. I'm also the woman who was instantly smitten when Sylvester Stallone, mid-interview, used the phrase "den of iniquity"—though that might say more about my love of multisyllabic words than anything else. (Also, Stallone is quite charming.) There was no denying that around Tom I had stopped just short of fanning myself like a Southern belle with the vapors. I fell asleep mildly worried that I would do something far worse over breakfast the next morning with Patrick Dempsey.

I got to the Chateau early and was shown to a somewhat secluded table on the patio, where I pondered the menu and wondered what one eats in the presence of a McDreamy. I wished there were a McMuffin or anything Mc-like on the menu so I could make a lame joke as an icebreaker. I knew it was probably pointless to order anything too filling—I had only one hour to cover the entire span of his career and comeback, as well as his personal life, and doubted I could do that and chomp through an omelet at the same time. I also knew I would inevitably just modulate my order to match Patrick's; no one would have to twist my arm to order some bacon if he was in the mood to eat a breakfast fit for a lumberjack.

But Patrick Dempsey certainly didn't need to order a ton of food to prove he was a man's man: every guy already wanted to be him, and every woman wanted to be with him, and as he walked toward me in the late-morning sunlight on the patio of the Chateau, it wasn't hard to see why. There was a certain amount of swagger, yes, but also an air of relaxed confidence that made everyone on the patio take notice. He offered me a firm handshake and a wry smile, then ordered herbal tea and some berries. Like I said, nothing to prove.

We talked about finding success on *Grey's*, and I was taken aback by how direct and almost blunt he was. "When the show first hit, I was just happy to have a job," he said of the *Grey's* gig, admitting that he had begun to consider becoming a full-time house-flipper until the role came along. "When I was unemployed for a while, people would say to me, 'You should focus on making independent movies.' And I'd say, 'No, I need a job that is going to pay me.' And I still feel that way. I don't want to go and make some film that five people will see in an art house. I have a family. I want to be a working actor. I want to make money. I don't see that there's anything wrong with that."

He then mentioned that he and his wife were thinking of expanding their family. "My wife would like to," he said, again surprising me with the fact that he wasn't really hiding his own reluctance to have more. "For me, if there was a way I could just get around those first six months, when the baby is screaming and crying and you can't make it stop, then I'd be fine," he said of contemplating life with a newborn. I later learned that in that moment, he was already aware, but was not yet revealing, that he and his wife were expecting twin boys. His knowledge of that may have led him to choose his words quite carefully. "We'll see what happens. Certainly, the clock is ticking," was all he said, with a shrug.

Maybe it was the fact that I was used to watching him effortlessly charm Meredith on *Grey's Anatomy* as opposed to his cool-as-a-cucumber demeanor now, or the fact that I couldn't remember the last time a star had been so straight and clear with his answers with only minimal spin attached. Maybe it was simply that in working for *Good Housekeeping* it was rare that I interviewed male stars, let alone two major ones in the space of twenty-four hours. Whatever the reason, I quickly realized my fears that I would dissolve into an eyelash-batting mess around Patrick Dempsey were not materializing. I might be a Star-Rhymes-with-Trucker, but apparently I'm still a selective one. I found it hard to feel Patrick and I were truly connecting. An actor's sex appeal is, of course, just as subjective as it is for anyone else: for every woman who adores Kevin Costner, there are others who fail to see his charms. I once had a twenty-minute argument with a colleague who insisted she would never sleep with Harrison Ford. (I counter that she's clearly never seen *Working Girl*. Or *Witness*.) But now Patrick Dempsey was seeming like one of those dog-whistle guys: others could hear it, but not me. As we left the restaurant that morning and I crossed in front of him, he put his hand on my arm briefly to guide me past a table. The inner super-fan in my head barely let out a whimper. "I don't know, I think I just don't get it," I later told Ellen about my resistance to swooning over him. "I guess he's not my type."

I now look back at my initial reaction and realize how

naïve I was. Because you know what Patrick Dempsey wasn't doing that morning at breakfast? Putting on an act. I had breakfast with Patrick Dempsey, and I had been waiting for McDreamy to show up.

A few weeks later, he did. We photographed Patrick at a downtown loft in New York City for the cover. I arrived just as he began posing for the camera. The heavy studio door made a loud scraping noise when I walked in, causing Patrick to look away from the lens he had been focusing his mega-watt smile towards, and instead turn that smile, so perfectly composed for the camera, directly on me. His eyes sparkled as he gave me a slight head nod of recognition. I suddenly felt my pulse quicken: this was the way he looked at Meredith Grey. This was the way he looked when he wanted you to swoon. This was him turning it on. "Oh," I thought to myself. "I get it now."

Patrick's wife, Jillian, a very successful hair and makeup artist, was also on set. At one point, she stepped in front of the camera for a moment to adjust his hair. He gazed up at her, and the look of total adoration she got was enough to make every single woman—and a few of the men—in the studio actually sigh a little bit. The photographer even shot the moment, and when we looked at the resulting picture, the look Patrick Dempsey is giving his wife is one of the purest, sexiest, and most romantic things I've ever seen. It was dreamier than McDreamy. It was so great we ran it in the magazine, even though it was just an outtake. Clearly, when Patrick Dempsey wants you to feel something, you'll feel it. While I would have enjoyed staring into his eyes over some bacon with him that morning at the Chateau, I nevertheless appreciated the fact that he'd had no desire to turn our breakfast into a charm offensive. (But I still wish he'd ordered bacon.)

To be honest, though, even if he had delivered his best McDreamy at breakfast, I'm not sure it would have worked. Because by the morning after the Le Meridien, my heart already belonged to another man.

The Tom Cruise cover story ran in *GH* roughly two months after my afternoon with him; by that time, Suri had been born. Returning home to my apartment one evening, there was a thick, bronze-colored envelope waiting on my doorstep. I opened it and inside was a handwritten note. It was a thank-you note from Tom. He praised the article in *GH* and let me know how much he'd enjoyed his time with me. Then, at the end, he added, *"Suri is sleeping peacefully next to me right now and it is impossible not to be filled with joy just looking at her. I hope you will give my best to your husband and that you are well. Sincerely, Tom."*

He had nothing left to gain; the story had already run. I can tell you that in my entire career, I can count on one hand the number of celebrities who have written me a thank-you note. There is only one who somehow managed to locate my home address and send it to me there. There is also only one who remembered to mention my husband. Of course I kept that note, and of course I still look at it from time to time. It's one of the classiest things I've ever seen a star do. Until, of course, Tom topped it.

Years later, I became a senior editor at *People*. Not long after I started, Tom Cruise agreed to do a cover story for the magazine. By now married to Katie Holmes for three years, he had continued to have successful films at the box office, but questions still dogged his relationship with Katie: Why hadn't they had another kid? Why did Suri never wear pants? Did Nicole Kidman ever see the kids she and Tom had adopted together, who now seemed to spend much of their time with Tom? Tom, still not afraid to speak his mind, agreed to do an interview to set the record straight.

People got the exclusive thanks to Jess Cagle, one of the magazine's executive editors at the time (and now its editorial director), who had a long professional history with Tom and had interviewed him multiple times in the past. It was clear that Jess would do the interview and, in an interesting twist, Tom asked if he could come to the *People* offices to do the piece. Celebrities stopping by *People* isn't exactly unheard of: Very often publicists will ask to bring their up-and-coming or making-a-comeback stars to our offices for what we call a "meet-and-greet." Massive A-list celebrities of Tom's caliber, however, didn't generally grace our halls. *People* was more than happy to welcome Tom, of course. Meanwhile, I secretly hoped that there might be some way our paths would cross while he was in the building. Of course, I knew better than to try to intrude on Jess's interview in any way, especially as I was still the new girl.

The day of Tom's interview, I was in the lobby of *People*'s offices after buying some lunch. As I was walking to the elevator, I could feel a palpable shift in the air—suddenly there were a flurry of whispers and a few not-so-subtly flashing camera phones. I turned around, and there was Jess, escorting his guest, Tom Cruise, into the elevator. Then Jess noticed me. "Kate! Come join us," Jess said, because he is the Greatest Kindest Man Alive. I got into the elevator with them, clutching my soup. Jess introduced me to Tom. Instantly, my babbling began. It was as if I had learned nothing from Mariska.

"Mr. Cruise, I don't suppose you remember me, but I actually interviewed you three years ago for the cover of *Good Housekeeping*, when you were promoting *Mission: Impossible III*. You were so generous with your time, and it was such a great interview for me. I remember Suri was about to be born..."

Tom beamed at me. "Of course! I remember you! It's great to see you again!" he smiled.

By now I at least knew enough not to believe that he really remembered me or our interview, at all. He was just being polite, surely. But then he paused for a moment and said the following:

"Your husband is a schoolteacher, right? He teaches younger kids? And he used to play football?"

I nodded, stunned. Just as I was trying to form words to express how amazed I was that he recalled anything about me, at all, Tom turned to Jess and began talking again.

"You gotta ask her sometime about how she met her husband," he said to Jess. "It's a fantastic story. They were camp counselors together, and then they were apart for years before he tracked her down and they reunited!"

I wish I could tell you how I replied but by that point my brain had exploded and was slowly trickling out of my ears. Oh, except this I do remember: when we got out of the elevator, he hugged me goodbye. I'm proud to report that I stopped hugging first, which was no small feat given that every fiber of my being wanted to cling to him like an orphaned koala.

I've told this story to people and they've said Tom

remembering the details of my life story must be due to some sort of Scientology mind trick that helps you recall everything you hear about somebody. Maybe. But if so, I don't care. He liked me enough to employ a Scientology mind trick on me in that case.

Really, though, I like to think it wasn't Scientology that made Tom hang on to my every word as much as it was his burgeoning love for me. Back then, the feeling was absolutely mutual; I am willing to bet it would have been for any woman with a pulse who spent two hours alone with him. Nevertheless, years later when I heard that Tom and Katie were splitting up, I was genuinely sad about the news. They had seemed very much in love. The real shame of it was that his timing couldn't have been worse: I'm still happily married, and really don't know if I'll ever be single again.

Chapter 6

Conan O'Brien Made Me Quit
(With an Assist from Dustin Hoffman)

MUCH HAS BEEN WRITTEN ABOUT THE TYPICAL traits of the only child, and I'm sure I embody the majority of them. I am ambitious and driven, and I have been known to howl if my husband reaches across a table to steal some of my macaroni and cheese (in other words, sharing can sometimes be an issue). But I generally play nicely with others, and for that I have my mother and Bethany Beach, Delaware, to thank.

My family spent two weeks on the Delaware coast every summer, a tradition that began when I was a mere toddler. I adored Bethany Beach, with one exception. The first day of any vacation was when one of the major drawbacks of being an only child came into sharp focus. Without a sibling, I had no built-in vacation companion, no friend to build forts with, no one to watch me attempt cartwheels in the sand. As a teen, I would bring a friend along on the trip, but before adolescence, I had to rely on my mother's solution to the problem.

Arriving on the beach that first morning, my mother would scan the surrounding blankets and umbrellas until she would spot her prey. Then, leaning down to me, she'd say, "There's a nice little girl over there, Katie. She's playing by herself. Why don't you go over there and say hi?"

I hated this moment, I hated walking over and saying hi, I hated being forced to go "make friends." Of course, it almost always worked: the little girl playing alone was also, often, an only child, or a child with older siblings who wanted nothing to do with her, or simply a really nice kid who was more than happy to attempt to do cartwheels with me. Once the connection was established, my family would return to that same spot on the sand each day and I would play with that same little girl, until the vacation ended. The next year, the process would repeat itself with a new girl, and a new friendship, which would never be maintained beyond those two weeks.

There was only one time I can recall that one of these attempted relationships went awry. A little girl named Leslie was my mother's suggested target that summer, yet Leslie herself turned out to be two years younger than I was, prompting me to later moan to my mom that I didn't want to spend the summer "playing with a baby." Leslie was only seven whereas I was all of nine. Yet Leslie had an older sister, Julie, who was a dazzling fourteen years old. Julie might as well have been Julia Roberts: that half decade she had over me made her impossibly exotic and effortlessly cool. While supposedly playing with Leslie I would orchestrate games that were thinly veiled excuses to join Julie's group of friends, which consisted of another teen girl and two teen boys. The four of them were often loitering underneath the beach houses built on stilts in the sand, and Leslie and I would show up, casually asking, "What are you guys doing? Can we play, too? Want to watch us do cartwheels?" They would sometimes let us join in whatever they'd been doing—leaping off dunes, mostly—but otherwise would yell at us to go away. I assumed it was Leslie's super-juvenile presence that prompted their rejection of us. But one afternoon I ventured under the beach houses without Leslie, who was busy having sunscreen reapplied by her mom.

I could see the teenagers lounging on a tire swing that someone had tied to the underside of the house, digging trenches in the sand with their feet. One of the boys noticed me approaching and spun around in the tire, facing Julie.

"Ugh, that girl is coming over here again," he said, not realizing (or not caring) that I was in earshot.

"Oh Jesus," Julie said with a sigh. "Can't she tell where she's not wanted?"

I turned and ran back to my family's beach blanket, then spent the rest of the week playing with Leslie—with whom I admittedly had much in common and who made an excellent Carrie Ingalls to my Laura. After that, I always made doubly sure that I was keeping company with people who wanted me there: I had no desire to stay too long at the party.

By the time I had been at *Good Housekeeping* for seven years, I'll admit, I had looked around for other jobs. All of them, however, were roughly the same song with different lyrics. Booking celebrities to be on the cover of *Cosmopolitan*. Booking celebrities to be on the cover of *Self*. Booking celebrities to attend the *Vanity Fair* Oscar party. What made my position at *Good Housekeeping* unique was—unlike the entertainment editor roles at many other magazines, which were purely about wrangling stars to appear in the issue and involved no editing or writing at all (so much so that many in that position will identify themselves solely as "a wrangler")—*GH* let me handle the interviews and, when I didn't do the interview myself, I edited the cover story. I enjoyed the editing as much as the writing, because if I wasn't the author, Liz Smith usually was. A living legend and a nationally syndicated gossip columnist whose work ran in the *New York Post*, Liz was under contract to *GH* and was the primary celebrity writer for the magazine. A straight-talking Texan with a cackling laugh, Liz had invited me to lunch not long after I started. By the end of the meal, she put her hand over mine and said, "Well, I can tell we're going to be great friends." She was eighty years old and my personal hero. Virtually no one said no to Liz, and she was the very best chance we had at getting reluctant celebrities to agree to be in the magazine. When all my pitches and pleading failed, letting a publicist know that none other than Liz Smith would be doing the interview could often make a star do an about-face and get on board.

It was easy to see why: whenever possible, Liz would conduct her interviews at Le Cirque, an iconic restaurant where, over the course of two or sometimes three hours, Liz and her celebrity guest would eat, drink, and talk about anything and everything. The next day, the transcript—hilarious, revealing, touching, and incredibly humanizing of the person she'd dined with—would land on my desk. I had the enviable task of taking thirty pages of banter, revelation, and warmth, and whittling it down to three thousand words. Someday those transcripts should all be bound together in a book and run in their entirety. (You're welcome, future publisher of *Lunches with Liz*. And Liz, I expect a cut of the profits.)

So if I wasn't interviewing Tom Cruise, I was editing Liz's transcript of her meal with Nicole Kidman. That alone was reason not to give serious thought to straying from *GH*. The other reason was Ellen Levine. After all those years, Ellen had taken me from a tabloid reporter in my early twenties and helped me grow into a seasoned journalist and editor. She had also witnessed my evolution from a single girl who would occasionally attend a meeting while nursing a hangover to a wife and mother who nursed two kids. Nearly every major adult milestone I experienced happened while I was at *GH*, and happened on Ellen's watch. (Full confession: her husband, Dr. Levine, is even my OB/GYN. How's that for bonding with your boss?) I had gotten married, I had become a mom, I had interviewed Jennifer Lopez and Jennifer Garner and Reese Witherspoon. Other than the thrill of a sexier magazine title on my business card, I wasn't sure why I would ever walk away from *Good Housekeeping*.

Then Ellen announced she was leaving.

To be fair, she wasn't going far. Having worked for decades for the Hearst Corporation, which owns *Good Housekeeping*, Ellen was rightfully being given the promotion of a lifetime: to Editorial Director of the entire company. She would still have some say about what happened at *Good Housekeeping*, but it would be but one of dozens of titles she would be overseeing. Day-to-day operations would be handled by the newly hired editor in chief, Rosemary Ellis.

I had never had a new boss at an old job before: everyone I had ever worked for had been the one to hire me. I realized that it was very possible Rosemary would arrive and instantly want to clean house and install an almost entirely new staff—it's a fairly common move for a new editor in chief. The only things I had going for me were Ellen's continued role at the company, and the fact that Rosemary was coming from *Prevention*, a health-oriented magazine that didn't focus much on celebrities. Ideally, this would mean that Rosemary didn't already have a roster of celebrity writers and wranglers she would want to bring on board and she would be willing to work with me.

It was clear to everyone on staff that Rosemary was radically different from Ellen. One anecdote that seems illustrative: Ellen had favored a springtime apple-green color that was basically the unofficial shade of the brand—at one point, the office's carpets and upholstery had even been in that shade, and it was used for the logo printed on all of our stationery and business cards. Rosemary reportedly took one look at the color on the cards and said, "Can we get rid of this green? Can we make it red?" Red and green: that's about as visual a contrast as I can give to convey the mere beginning of their differences.

In many ways, I understood exactly where Rosemary was coming from. She, no doubt, wanted to shake up the brand, make it sexier, edgier, and more approachable. It was exactly what I had wanted to do when I first started trying to lure celebrities to the magazine. And Rosemary meant business: forget about worrying if Jennifer Lopez was too racy for the readership. In Rosemary's first year, she ran an erotic poem called "Fusion" in the magazine, written by Lana Holstein, a doctor and sex expert. I wouldn't be surprised if readers were still writing in about it. I admired all the ways in which Rosemary wanted the magazine to be different, fresher, and younger. I had also, over seven years, come to learn all the ways in which I needed to make the already established elements of the brand—the trust, the reputation, the massive reach—work for me, rather than trying to bend the brand until it broke. I felt I knew which wars were worth fighting.

But Rosemary had a different battle plan. For starters, she expressed a clear interest in attending all the celebrity photo shoots that took place—a role normally left to me and the magazine's art director, and something that Ellen had never considered doing. Rosemary also said she would occasionally be the one to conduct the celebrity interview. Though that was also hardly the norm, Rosemary was certainly well within her rights to want to do these things: she was in charge. I consoled myself with the knowledge that at least I was still the primary editor for the cover stories, regardless of who wrote them.

One such story came in just a few weeks after Rosemary had started. Before her arrival, we had promised Katie Couric the November cover, pegged to her upcoming debut as the anchor of the *CBS Evening News*. I hadn't opted to do the interview myself, nor was it one that seemed the right fit for

Liz Smith, as she mainly focused on major TV and movie stars. Instead, I'd turned to the roster of experienced female writers we had on contract. In this case, I had given the assignment to a veteran journalist I worked with frequently, and I had guided her through the various talking points I wanted her to be sure to hit with Katie.

The writer wound up spending a full day with Katie, traveling with her in a Town Car to and from appointments and attending our photo shoot. The result was a first draft that was, understandably, a bit unwieldy: like the hours spent with Katie, it ranged far and wide and occasionally lost focus or needed to be clarified and reigned in. I spent several hours overhauling the draft and talking with the author about a few additions I thought needed to be made. Then, the next day, Rosemary called me into her office.

Sitting there already was Evelyn Renold, the deputy editor who often gave a final edit to my cover stories. In my early years at *GH*, Evelyn had truly shaped me into an editor by being such an impeccable one herself, going through my early drafts line by line with me, pencil in hand, and patiently explaining what should be changed. Over the years, I had become able to hear Evelyn in my head as I wrote, advising me on the best introduction sentences or conclusions. More importantly, I consistently used what I had learned from her as I edited other writers: never rewriting someone but rather reworking, shaping, and polishing what was already there.

After a few minutes in her office, it became clear that Rosemary had also seen the first draft of the Couric story, and had called this meeting to deliver her notes on it to me and Evelyn. I began jotting them down, waiting for the right moment to interject that I had actually already completed one fairly thorough edit. Then Rosemary turned to Evelyn and said, "So let me know when you have a clean first draft and we'll see if we need to go back to Katie."

I looked at Evelyn and Rosemary in confusion. "I've actually already done an edit..." I began.

"That's okay, Evelyn's got this," Rosemary replied then turned her chair back to the computer. It was clear she had no interest in seeing any revision I might have done.

"So...I don't need to have edited this?" I said, baffled.

"Right," Rosemary said pleasantly. "Evelyn's handling it."

I fell silent. Afterward, Evelyn seemed baffled by what had happened. I had a pretty strong idea. To Rosemary, I was just a wrangler. Even worse, I was now starting to suspect that perhaps she wanted to remove me after all, regardless of whether or not she had someone else lined up for my job.

The next month, a Martha Stewart interview I had negotiated and secured for the cover was scheduled. I was worried Martha might not be loose enough for lunch with Liz, plus I adored Martha's style, and was a longtime fan. Evelyn had encouraged me to consider doing the interview myself. "She'll never see you coming," she said. "She won't be suspicious of you if you want to ask some tougher questions." I found myself excited to take on the challenge.

By the end of the day, however, I got word that Rosemary wanted the same author who had written the Couric piece to handle Martha. She didn't want me to do it, or for Liz to do it, either. Once again, I was out.

Meanwhile, Rosemary did have other ways in which she wanted me involved. She had a vision for a new section to run in the beginning pages of the magazine—what's referred to as the "front of the book"—that would be entirely celebrity-oriented. The section would be called Good Buzz, as part of an ongoing initiative to rebrand several sections of the magazine with the word "Good," as a play off our title. We now had Good Advice, Good Looks, Good Food, and Good Health sections, among others. She wanted the opening pages to include a quick look at a celebrity style trend, and a quote from a celebrity about motherhood, and maybe a one-page interview with a star.

I suggested the star always be male—we still so rarely featured male celebrities in the magazine—and offered the title Man of the House for the page, as a nod to the second half of our title. Rosemary was enthusiastically on board. She was also fine with me doing the quick phone interviews that accompanied the page (which meant I wound up bantering on the phone with Pierce Brosnan, swooning on the phone over Kyle Chandler, and almost accidentally hanging up the phone on Steve Carell when he made me laugh uncontrollably). Most amazingly, she signed off on a four-day work week for me when I asked for more time with my kids. Not even a work-from-home-one-day-a-week deal: a true four-day work week, in which I fully and completely had Friday off. Yet my paycheck was unchanged. I want to stress this repeatedly—*fewer days, same money*—because even if I were now to tell you I was also subjected to regular beatings (which I most certainly was not), that fact right there—*fewer days, same money*—makes Rosemary Ellis hands down one of the most gracious and generous bosses I have ever had.

So, Rosemary wanted me to focus much of my attention on Good Buzz rather than writing or editing larger cover stories (though she still wanted me to book the celebrities for those). I had previously spent the majority of my time wrangling one star per month to appear on the cover, plus occasionally lining up a celebrity for a fashion, beauty, or home story inside, and here or there writing a shorter profile on someone who was either up-and-coming or making a comeback. At most, I had been working on getting three celebrities into the magazine every month and then overseeing those stories by writing and editing them, and that was a full-time endeavor. Now, in addition to continuing to get stars for the cover, Good Buzz would require at least eight or more additional celebrities to participate with the magazine every month. Just getting one or two yeses each month had been daunting. Now I needed nearly a dozen.

As the section began to shape up, I started to develop strategies for how to fill the space. One regular feature was a spotlight on how a star was giving back: I contacted countless charities that had A-list supporters and worked with them to get a quote from a celebrity about why that cause was close to their heart. The style feature was created by looking at red carpet trends, and was curated by the magazine's fashion director, to whom I was profoundly grateful. The quote on motherhood which opened the section was generally something that was picked up from previous interviews a star had given, meaning no begging of publicists was required. Man of the House took some wrangling and time, but I found it was far easier to sell men on the idea of appearing in *Good Housekeeping*, as they had no qualms that the title made them seem old or frumpy and instead were eager to reach twenty-five million movie-going, TV-watching, album-buying females.

That left just one part of the section as a true challenge: the recipe. Rosemary wanted to run a celebrity-created recipe every single month, and while it sounded simple, it proved to be a huge headache. Asking publicists if one of their clients would provide a recipe to *GH* was only a few steps removed from asking them to appear on the cover in an apron while holding a mixing bowl: for many A-listers, it precisely evoked the dowdy, overly domestic image that had made them dubious about *Good Housekeeping* in the first place. Some stars were willing, sure—country stars proved particularly game. Still, it became clear that coming up with options month after month was going to be a challenge, especially since not just any recipe would do; it needed to be seasonally appropriate (green-bean casserole for Thanksgiving, BBQ in the summertime).

Thankfully, the Internet came to my rescue. Thousands of celebrity cookbooks have been published, and even more celebrity recipes had found their way onto websites. As long as the cookbook's publisher was properly notified and credited, *GH* was generally able to reprint those recipes. As for recipes that lived primarily online, I developed a strategy there as well. I quickly learned that openly asking for permission to run a recipe when in fact I didn't actually need such permission (as long as the recipe had already run and we credited it properly) was a surefire way to get a publicist to say no. If publicists *could* say no to *GH*, more often than not, they *would*.

However, if I made it clear, in writing, that I was not actually asking for permission but instead was merely informing them of our decision as a courtesy, I often would receive no objection. The form letter I ultimately sent out each month read like this:

Dear Publicist Name Here,

Hope you've been doing well since the Emmys/your wedding/your maternity leave/your vacation/our horrible winter/whatever vague moment we last shared! I wanted to give you a quick head's up that we're going to pick up a recipe for Celeb Name Here's Fried Chicken that previously ran on Website Name Here, and use it in our August issue. If for some reason that poses a problem (say, because Celeb Name is now a vegan or something?) just let me know. If I do not hear back from you, I will assume we're okay to proceed.

> Thanks so much, Publicist Name.
> Hope we can get together soon!
> Kate

Pay careful attention to that sentence: *If I do not hear back from you, I will assume we're okay to proceed.* Because it turned out to be one of the stupidest things I've ever written, and it's not something I will ever, in the rest of my career, write again.

One of the other ways I made the added workload of Good Buzz manageable was to book as much as possible well in advance. In general, monthly magazines operate three months ahead of time, so that the November issue is being worked on in August, the October issue in July, and so on. December meant it was time to start putting together the March issue. And a March issue meant a St. Patrick's Day theme.

Years earlier, back in 2004, it had been announced that Conan O'Brien was going to be the new host of *The Tonight Show* in 2009. By late 2007, Conan had already begun the process of moving some of his staff from New York City across the country to Los Angeles, where *The Tonight Show* would continue to be filmed. Many of his handlers were in flux: some were following him, others staying behind to work on *Late Night* with the new incoming host, Jimmy Fallon. Within roughly the same time frame, Conan's longtime publicist had expanded and renamed her company, complete with new e-mail addresses. Oh, and did I mention it was the holidays, when most people in the industry take the week between Christmas and New Year's off?

This is all relevant because I had located what I thought was the perfect recipe for the March issue. Conan O'Brien's St. Patrick's Day Stew. Simple enough—meat, potatoes, carrots—but we rarely got a recipe from a man, and what's more, this one was thematically appropriate. The recipe had appeared on a well-known and seemingly reputable content-aggregation site (in other words, a site which reposted stories and articles that had appeared elsewhere on the web; think *Huffington Post*, only this was before the *Huffington Post*) and I tracked it back to several other newspapers that had run it as well. I sent off my standard recipe form letter both to the address I believed to be the correct one for Conan's publicist, as well as to Conan's show representatives, and I waited. When I heard nothing after a few weeks, I had the food department make and double-check the recipe, as I did every month, and proceeded to finish the March edition of Good Buzz.

Three months later, I came into my office a few days after the March issue had gone on sale. My assistant at the time looked unusually excited to see me.

"You're not going to believe who called," she said eagerly. "Conan O'Brien's office! They want a few copies of the March issue to be sent over to the show."

In that very instant I knew: something had gone horribly wrong. The chances that Conan wanted copies of the magazine to share with his family and friends were slim to none. The fact that it wasn't his personal publicist who had called but rather a producer for the show made it abundantly clear that something about the recipe was going to be used as fodder for that night's episode.

"Don't call back," I told my assistant. "Don't send them anything, either." As if that was really going to stop what happened next.

I stayed awake until 12:35 that night, practically holding my breath. Conan went through his entire monologue and made not one mention of St. Patrick's Day Stew. When the show went to a commercial, I began to exhale. Maybe he'd thought better of it? Maybe I was overreacting? Maybe nothing was going to happen at all?

And then the show came back from commercial.

Conan was seated at his desk, and I saw immediately that the March copy was in front of him.

"Folks, I was sitting in hair and makeup this afternoon, and so I was reading my latest issue of *Good Housekeeping*, as I do," he said, holding up the issue. The idea that Conan read *Good Housekeeping* regularly got a big laugh from the audience.

"Imagine my surprise, though, as I was thumbing through my copy, to find a recipe for Conan O'Brien's St. Patrick's Day Stew," he said, lapsing into an Irish accent.

He quickly detailed what was involved in the recipe, then looked directly at the camera.

"Except here's the thing, folks: This is not my recipe. I can't even make ramen noodles. I've never made anything like this before in my life," he said. "I can only assume that *Good Housekeeping* needed some Irish fathead to represent a St. Patrick's Day recipe, so they made this up and put me on there. They must've used Ted Kennedy last year."

The audience was howling, but I felt physically ill. We hadn't simply made up the recipe, no, but I now saw all too well the fallacy in my fact-checking method with his publicist. Worst of all, Conan was still talking.

"I would just like to ask the good people at *Good House-keeping* if maybe they could send me some of this stew? I mean, after all, since it's apparently me saintly grandmother's recipe," he said, returning to the Irish accent, "I sure would appreciate tasting a wee bit of it."

With that, he moved on to his next segment, and I spent the rest of the early morning hours alternating between tears and terror.

The next morning, I immediately called the publicist for *GH*, a woman roughly my age who regularly accompanied me when I made appearances on TV to talk about that month's issue. I explained to her what I had now realized must have happened: my e-mailed form letter had flown into a perfect storm of typical holiday absences coupled with a situation where neither Conan's publicist nor his usual show handler was at their old e-mail address anymore. The publicist was in charge of making sure *Good Housekeeping* got good press—which this decidedly was not. Yet she seemed surprisingly sanguine about the situation.

"Really, this is the most talked-about *Good Housekeeping* has been in years," she said with a laugh. "We're going to put out a statement apologizing and saying we believed that the recipe came from a respectable and trustworthy source and that through a series of miscommunication errors, we thought that it had been verified. It will be fine."

Rosemary, however, was significantly less calm about the matter, and understandably so. Conan's riff had been picked up by a few websites, all using clever headlines about *Not-So-Good Housekeeping* and wittily asking "What do Ramen and St. Patrick's Day Stew Have in Common? Conan O'Brien Can't Make Either." Rosemary didn't call me into her office; instead, she walked into mine and closed the door behind her.

"This is not good. It is really not good," she said, glaring. I had never wanted to dive under my desk more.

"Rosemary, I am so *so* sorry. I wish I could say that I don't know how this happened but now, in hindsight, I do, and I am just so sorry and I swear to you this will not happen, ever again," I said, groveling as much as I could without actually falling to my knees, though I considered it briefly.

"Oh, I know it won't," Rosemary replied pointedly. I then swung into recovery mode.

"I'm trying to think of ways to fix this," I said. "I'm going to talk to the show today and also his publicist and I'll tell you everything they say."

"I want to know exactly who you're talking to," Rosemary said, which I understood since she no longer had any reason to be confident that I knew how to reach the right people. I told her the name of the publicist for *Late Night* who was still in place, as well as Conan's personal rep, whose new e-mail and phone number I now knew by heart.

"Make sure you get both of them to understand we didn't just make this up," she said at last. I nodded frantically in agreement. She got up to go, but turned to look at me one last time.

"This is really, really not good," she said, and then left.

I dove for my phone and called the *Late Night* publicist, a nice-enough guy whom I had only ever talked to a handful of times in the past when I'd needed tickets to the show. Sure enough, he had no idea I'd ever e-mailed; I had previously reached out to someone who was already in a new position in preparation for *The Tonight Show*.

"Please, please, you have to help me," I begged him.

"Oh, relax, it was just one bit. No one even cares," he said, trying to be reassuring.

"Oh sweet Christ, I care! And you'd better believe my boss cares," I practically shouted. "But look, I have an idea."

I began to lay out my plans—because I now had more than one.

"Conan said he wanted *Good Housekeeping* to send him some stew. We will totally do that! My boss, Rosemary Ellis, will come on air and serve him some stew on a silver platter. Listen to me: Literally, on a silver platter. She will spoon-feed it to him if he wants. Seriously."

I heard the publicist chuckle a bit and took it as a sign to proceed.

"Okay and, also, Conan should totally come here to the Good Housekeeping Institute, where we make the recipes and do everything else! Yes, the Good Housekeeping Institute is real!"

Perhaps the most famous thing about *Good Housekeeping* is the venerable Good Housekeeping Seal of Approval. It is an emblem placed on products that guarantees the product will perform as promised, and provides a limited warranty to consumers offering a replacement or refund if the product is defective. The Seal of Approval is a sign of tried-and-tested quality. That testing takes place in an actual institute—The Good Housekeeping Institute, located one floor above the magazine's editorial offices. No product could receive the seal without being put through the wringer, sometimes literally. In addition to test kitchens where recipes were perfected and taste tests conducted, there were humidity chambers for testing hair products and moisture resistance, machines that stretched and twisted fabrics, hydraulic presses that tested an object's durability, climate-controlled rooms that determined flammability, and more rooms and areas and gadgets than an English major like me could possibly understand. Actual chemists worked at the Institute. With its sleek white halls and glass-walled rooms, behind which cookies were being made and suitcases were being blasted and vacuum cleaners being pulled apart, the Institute was like a cross between Willy Wonka's Chocolate Factory and a set from *2001: A Space Odyssey*. I knew Conan would have a field day if we let him loose in there.

"Please, invite him!" I begged the *Late Night* publicist. "We would love to have him!"

He promised to run both ideas by Conan and get back to me as soon as he heard anything. I hung up and practically sprinted to Rosemary's office. I explained both ideas to her, and said that the *Late Night* rep had seemed very responsive.

"Who exactly did you pitch these ideas to?" she asked. I gave her the name of Conan's show publicist, and she told me to keep her posted. I went back to my office and waited. It was a Tuesday.

The next day, when I hadn't heard back from *Late Night*, I wasn't overly concerned. I knew it could take a day or so for the publicist to get an answer from Conan or his writers, and part of me thought that it might be better in the end for the story to simply die. I also noticed Rosemary didn't call or e-mail me throughout the entire day, and I chose to be grateful for that rather than worried that it meant she was silently seething.

But the next day, when I still hadn't heard from *Late Night*, I hesitated before calling to follow up. Maybe, by this point, two days after the fact, Rosemary would rather the matter stay dormant. I walked over to her office to check with her, but found it empty.

"Do you know when Rosemary will be back?" I asked her assistant.

"Oh, I don't know if she's coming back today. She left for the studio about an hour ago, and I don't think the taping will be done until after six," her assistant replied. Then she frowned at me.

"Shouldn't you have gone to the studio with her?" she asked. "I'm surprised she didn't bring you."

I took a deep breath, and decided not to pretend that I'd been clued in at all.

"I have no idea what you're talking about," I said, then realized I'd misspoken. I did have an idea. "Is the studio you're talking about...Conan O'Brien's studio? Is she over there filming a segment?"

"Yes!" her assistant said happily. "Isn't that amazing! She's going to be on the show tonight!"

I smiled weakly and walked back to my office. I called the publicist for *Late Night*, but there was no answer. I called the publicist for the magazine, but there was also no answer—she was likely accompanying Rosemary to the show.

I was truly stymied as to why Rosemary wouldn't have at least told me that my idea had been successful, and that in fact this entire fiasco was resulting in perhaps the hippest, most youthful publicity the magazine had gotten in decades, if not ever. Just then, the *Late Night* publicist returned my call.

"You could've told me that you were having my boss on!" I practically shouted at him, effectively misplacing my frustration.

"Hey, don't yell at me," he said jovially. "Take it up with your boss—she and I connected directly the day after you called me! Didn't she tell you?"

I thanked him for having Rosemary appear on the show and got off the phone as quickly as I could. My hands were shaking, and random moments from the past months I had spent working for Rosemary were coming to mind. Katie

Couric. Martha Stewart. Now this. A small voice somewhere inside me whispered, *"Can't you tell where you're not wanted?"*

I did what I often do when my brain tells me something I don't want to hear: I thought about food. I had a party to attend that weekend and had promised to bring homemade cupcakes. The only problem was, I didn't have a muffin tin. Suddenly desperate to leave my office, I decided to head up to the Institute's test kitchens and see if I could borrow one.

Upstairs, the Institute was more spotless and organized than I had ever seen it before. I found the food director, Susan, in one of the kitchens, and as she handed me a muffin pan, I asked her why everything was so neat and tidy.

"Oh, well, you know, we were told that the camera crews are going to need room to set up, and we didn't want to have the usual clutter lying around so we swung into action..." Susan began. I had thought my heart couldn't sink any lower, but it somehow found a sub-basement.

"Camera crews? Who's coming to film here?" I asked quietly, although I fully knew the answer.

"Conan O'Brien!" Susan said excitedly. "He's filming a segment up here tomorrow where he's going to get a tour of the whole place from Rosemary. Didn't she tell you?"

I simply smiled, weakly again, and went back downstairs to my desk. The voice in my head was louder: *"Do you get it now?"*

I've gotten a lot of useful advice from my mother about being a woman in a workplace. Never cry in the office. Don't go to someone with your problems unless you're also bringing your solutions. And most crucially: never leave a job until you have a job. I had no idea whether Rosemary's latest exclusion of me was just one more step toward inevitably having me replaced or if it was some form of punishment. But I was no longer interested in waiting around to find out.

I suddenly thought of the famous scene in *Kramer vs. Kramer*, when Dustin Hoffman, unemployed and desperately trying to win custody of his son, is told by his attorney that having a job before they go to court the next day is an imperative. That afternoon, Hoffman goes on a job interview, and when the men hiring try to humor him by saying they'll be in touch in a few weeks, Hoffman snaps. "No. This is a one-day-only offer, Gentlemen. You're going to have to let me know today," he insists.

My phone rang, and I glanced at it before picking up, almost letting it go to voice mail. But it was Cindi Berger, a legendary publicist, a woman I had long adored and who only represented serious mega-stars. I knew better than to screen her.

"Hey," I said tersely, doing a miserable job at masking my mood. Cindi, it should also be noted, was not just a legendary publicist but also a Jewish mother of the highest order— an ultra-nurturer who made it her personal mission to care for her clients and other people she liked as though she had birthed them herself. I was about to learn I was lucky enough to be counted among them.

"Oh my god, what is the matter with you?" she asked upon hearing my voice.

I hesitated, and thought for only the briefest second of telling her the whole story. Instead, I settled on the most important aspect of it.

"Honestly? I need a new job. Desperately. I need a new job, like, yesterday. It's time for me to go. Like, right now, *today*," I said, doing my best to channel Dustin Hoffman. "Listen, promise me, if you hear of any openings anywhere, will you let me know? I mean *anywhere*. If you hear that *Field & Stream* is hiring, you call me."

Cindi gasped.

"Oh my god," she said. "This is insane. I had lunch today with Larry Hackett, an old friend of mine and the editor of *People* magazine, and I swear to god I was talking about you! He needs someone, ideally with a woman's magazine background, as a senior editor over there. I said you would be perfect but that I didn't think in a million years he could get you because you've been at *Good Housekeeping* for so long you must be really happy there. Oh my god!"

I abandoned all decorum.

"Now you listen to me," I said, sounding less like Hoffman now and more like Liam Neeson in *Taken*. "You call Larry Hackett right now and tell him I am ripe for the picking. You tell him I will be calling him within the hour and I will do anything, anything, if he will just take my call."

"Oh, honey," Cindi laughed. "He's gonna take your call. I'll make sure of it."

We hung up, and a mere twenty minutes later, she called me back.

"Call him now," she said. "He's expecting you."

I called, and when Larry picked up, he said in his inimitable, clarion voice, "So, I hear maybe you and I should meet?"

"Yes, please," I replied.

That night, Rosemary Ellis appeared on *Late Night with Conan O'Brien*, where she walked on stage carrying a bowl of St. Patrick's Day Stew on a silver platter. She sat next to

Conan at his desk and bantered with him good-naturedly, while he declared the stew was good but not Irish enough for his liking and proceeded to add Jameson Irish Whiskey, Baileys Irish Cream, and finally a box of Lucky Charms cereal to it, as Rosemary tossed back her head and laughed.

The next day, Conan came and taped a segment at the Institute, where he was subjected to various tests, including a trip to the climate-controlled humidity chamber which made his hair look like an orange soufflé. Rosemary was by his side the entire time, playing the straight woman to his antics.

I wasn't there. Thanks to Rosemary, I had Fridays off. I also was busy meeting Larry Hackett in his office. He showed me to a seat on his couch, then sat across from me and asked, "So, what can I do for you?" In that moment, I discovered that one great thing about having the worst happen is that you no longer have anything to lose. It was Hoffman time.

"You could hire me. I really would love to work here. I think maybe I *need* to work here," I said, and Larry seemed pleased by my directness. Pleased enough that two weeks later, after several more meetings and a lengthy edit test, he called me again.

"So, you still want to come work for me?" he asked.

"Yes, please," I replied.

I had been at *Good Housekeeping* for eight and a half years, had written over thirty cover stories, and had edited nearly a hundred others. When I broke the news to Rosemary that I was leaving, she surprised me by actually making a feeble attempt to talk me out of it.

"I feel like you still have things to learn here," she offered.

Ultimately, she wished me well and even gave me a hug.

We actually had lunch on my second-to-last day at *GH*. She was warmer than I had ever found her during the time I'd spent working for her, and I wondered if our relationship would have been any different had she been the one to hire me in the first place.

But neither one of us promised to stay in touch.

Chapter 7

George Michael Is My Absolute Favorite
(Sorry, Not Sorry)

I HAD KNOWN I WOULD BE HAPPY AT *PEOPLE* IF
for no other reason than it was a fresh start after eight years
at *Good Housekeeping*. What I hadn't counted on was how
quickly I would feel at home there.

On my first day, I was shown to my new office, which was
empty except for a desk, chair, some shelves...and a television set. This was a thrill. Of course, at the *Post*, there had
been a few televisions dotted throughout the newsroom; we
generally only glanced at them during major breaking news
events, and even then, only briefly. ("Come on, the TV guys
are always the last to know anything," one metro desk editor would sneer if anyone lingered for too long.) In my final
years at *GH*, my computer had been able to stream certain

television stations, but it was the dawn of such technology and more often than not I was stuck staring at a frozen, pixilated image that was endlessly buffering.

Now I took a seat at my new desk and stared for a moment at the TV, cable box, and DVD player. Despite feeling a sort of free-floating anxiety, I cautiously turned it on. I half-expected it to be dead—a relic left behind by the office's previous occupant that maintenance workers had yet to clear away, perhaps. Instead, the TV hummed to life with the glorious vision of the E! channel, and Giuliana Rancic was discussing the latest celebrity breakup.

I began flipping between Giuliana on E! and Kathie Lee and Hoda Kotb hosting the third hour of the *Today* show when my new boss, Larry, walked by and stuck his head into my office. I quickly scrambled for the remote and tried to shut the TV off, but found myself nervously stabbing random buttons instead.

"How's it going?" Larry asked.

"Um...fine," I said, flustered and feeling guilty before confessing. "Sorry...you just busted me watching TV. Sorry."

"That's part of your job," Larry said. "Why do you think you have a TV in here? Don't apologize." Then he sauntered off down the hall.

The saying is that if you find a way to get paid to do what you love, then you'll never work a day in your life. Getting hired as the senior editor for television, I realized, meant I was now literally getting paid to know everything about TV—the one thing that had always come naturally to me. Loving my job would be easy.

The "not apologizing" part would take a little more time.

Being a teenager in the late 1980s and early 1990s meant coming of age during a perfect moment for moody, contemplative, complaint pop. R.E.M. wailed about losing their religion and everybody hurting while Edie Brickell sang virtually incomprehensible lyrics about being choked in shallow water. Just when the whining got to be overwhelming, Kurt Cobain and Nirvana and the rest of the grunge movement arrived on the scene to add some rage and angst to the proceedings. Revolutionary? Sure. Upbeat? Not exactly. Still, it was what every single one of my classmates was listening to, and while I gamely went to Tower Records and bought my 10,000 Maniacs and the Cure cassettes, I felt like an impostor the entire time. The truth was, my musical tastes were a lot more aligned with those of the two people I spent the most time with: my parents.

Running a theatrical advertising agency meant that my mother listened to a lot of original Broadway cast recordings. As a result, I was perhaps the only seven-year-old in New York City who could sing every last song from *Guys and Dolls*—even though I'd never been to the show. Years later, I would arrive at Oxford and begin studying T. S. Eliot, only to be pleasantly surprised to find that I already felt intimately familiar with many of his poems—because I still remembered every lyric from *Cats*.

My father, on the other hand, was one of seven kids born and raised in the macho-, hipster-sounding town of Mitchell, South Dakota. Rather than winding up with a career somehow tied to agriculture like many who went before him (my grandfather sold tractor parts, and one of my uncles is the dairy king of South Dakota), my dad left the state for college in Minnesota, then graduate school in Washington, DC, then tried his hand as an actor in New York City. When that didn't pan out, he landed in advertising. Perhaps to compensate for his more rural beginnings, he took his degrees in English (BA) and Drama (MA) seriously, and wielded the vocabulary to prove it. Imploring me to keep my voice down when visiting a museum, he'd say, "Let's all try to remain *sotto voce*," while I heaved an exasperated sigh. Objecting to a rather saucy front-page headline the *Post* ran while I worked there, he called to complain: "Getting rather concupiscent with the cover language, don't you think?" he asked. My favorite was the moment when he noticed a Christmas decoration that featured a Santa Claus tugging on Rudolph's reins, as Rudolph's head bucked back and forth. "Oh, look at Santa with the recalcitrant reindeer," he commented. Born in 1936, my dad felt truly great music was the kind written by Cole Porter and the Gershwins. (Listen to Annie Lennox sing "Every Time We Say Goodbye" and it's hard to disagree.) This is why I was probably the only thirteen-year-old who knew all the words to "Don't Get Around Much Anymore" and whose idea of a fantastic new album was the latest release from Carly Simon or Linda Ronstadt.

The closest I came to breaking away from the Lite FM preferences of my parents was when I discovered an adorable British pop duo who called themselves Wham! Unfortunately, I "discovered" them about two years after they'd broken up. No matter: by the time I'd thoroughly exhausted every single song on all three of their albums, George Michael was ready to launch his solo career with his new album, *Faith*.

The album was, of course, massive. Every song, every

video—from "I Want Your Sex" to "Father Figure"—became a huge hit. Unless, that is, you were walking the halls of the exclusive, obnoxious, private high school I attended. There, my fellow freshmen would openly declare that George Michael was a "loser" (and I'm ashamed to admit names far worse than that were used) and deemed his ballads—like the exquisite "One More Try"—to be "so totally lame."

Meanwhile, I was the girl screaming myself hoarse at the *Faith* tour when George played the Meadowlands arena in New Jersey. My date for the evening was the head writer at my mother's advertising agency, a fantastic, openly gay man whom I secretly wanted to marry someday. That is, right after I married George. Clearly, I was developing a type.

I never told anyone at school that I'd gone to the concert; I wouldn't have dared reveal that I adored George to any of my classmates. Besides, it's not like listening to George on my Walkman, rather than, say, Echo & the Bunnymen, was a huge burden to conceal. Secretly loving George Michael was hardly worthy of discussion. Until, during one magical vacation, it was.

Every year during either Thanksgiving or February break, my parents tried to escape the frigid New York winters and take a vacation with me that involved sand and sun. Most years, the trip was to the US Virgin Islands, where we regularly stayed at a place called Caneel Bay—which at the time was a fairly simple family resort without so much as a swimming pool, but which is now considerably more high-end with not only a pool but also a five-star spa. In 1990, my mother and I were enjoying what passed as one of the major activities at Caneel: floating on yellow foam mats in the middle of the gin-clear water. Then my father came paddling over, and promptly declared that the biggest pop star in the universe was now staying just two doors down.

"I think that guy you like so much is staying here, Katie," he said. "You know the one with the stubble—George Michaels?"

I had two reasons for bursting into laughter: First, there was absolutely no way that George Michael was staying at a tiny child-friendly resort in the not-exactly-ultra-chic US Virgin Islands. (St. Barths or Mustique it is not.) Second, the last person in the world who would be able to accurately recognize George Michael was my father. My dad could be relied upon to regularly misidentify civilians as celebrities. Living on the Upper West Side of Manhattan, less than a mile away from the famed former residence of John Lennon, meant that my father was certain nearly any short Asian woman who passed us on the street was, in fact, Yoko Ono. (It was almost always the woman who sold us fruit at the corner bodega.) Similarly, multiple brunettes over six feet tall were identified by my dad as Sigourney Weaver. He never, *ever* got it right. "Look—isn't that Bill Murray?" Dad exclaimed one afternoon, as I turned to look at the tall veterinarian with a receding hairline who actually lived one floor below us in our apartment building.

I knew better than to think for even a nanosecond that my father was right about George staying on the same beach as us.

"Dad," I said, exhaling dramatically. "There is no way George Michael is here. This place is all families. I don't know who you just saw—some guy with a five o'clock shadow, probably—but there's no way it was George Michael." My mom paddled over and I told her of Dad's latest "celebrity sighting." She hooted and confirmed there was no chance George Michael could be staying there. My dad just shrugged.

That night at dinner, I left my parents' table to join a group of jaded, world-weary teens who alternated between welcoming me as one of them and talking over my head to prove their superiority. Most of them were also from New York, went to obnoxious and exclusive high schools similar to mine, and were several years older than I was. But since we would never see each other again outside of this island and this resort, there was no real reason for them to exclude me. I was generally welcome to join them as they played ping-pong and tried to sneak beer, but I constantly felt as though I were walking a razor-thin ledge, trying desperately to keep from dropping into the chasm of the uncool. That night, as we flopped over several lounge chairs discussing the latest thing we found stupid, one of the teens, a girl named Amy with long, flawless blond hair I envied, rolled over and propped herself up on her elbows.

"Ewwww, guys, did I tell you what I heard?" she said with a half-yawn. "George Michael is staying here. So lame."

A boy named Max, whose acne-riddled skin apparently did nothing to temper his swaggering sense of self-confidence, let out a derisive snort. "Yeah, my mom said she heard he and his pal were staying at some other resort but people were like, constantly harassing them or whatever, so they came here instead," he explained. "He's gross. Who would even care where he was staying?"

"I heard he wants, like, total privacy," Amy the Blonde was continuing. "Tonight they closed down the beach bar so him and his guest could have dinner there. God, why does he have to be the one staying here? I wish it was someone cool like Michael Stipe or Morrissey."

I was now sitting up straight, my mind spinning. George Michael really was here? On the same beach where I was? There was no debate to be had: I had to go to wherever he was. Immediately. Declaring that I needed to leave to hunt down my favorite star in the universe was not going to be an acceptable exit line with this group, however.

"Um...I just forgot I have to tell my mom something about...um, a project I forgot I have to finish when I get back to school," I said, desperately.

"Whatever," Amy the Blonde said, cracking her gum.

I raced back to my parents' table.

"Ohmigod ohmigod ohmigod," I hissed to my mom and dad as I reached them, before saying a sentence my father has probably heard less than a dozen times in his life.

"Dad, you were right," I said. "George Michael is here! He's here right now! He's down in the beach bar and oh my god! If I don't get his autograph I am absolutely going to die. I have to *see him.*"

"You see! I told you!" my father said triumphantly. Perhaps it was his elation at having been correct that led to what he did next, as my mother waited for the check and I went back to the cool kids.

"Um, yeah, bad news...I gotta go back to the room with my parents. It's my grandmother's birthday and we promised to call her," I said. Absolutely no one seemed sorry to see me go, a fact which might have mortified me had I not been consumed with the task at hand: making my way to George. By then, my father was already fully on the case.

Finding George had proved remarkably easy: he and his friend, finished with dinner and now enjoying a few drinks and some quiet conversation, were still seated in the otherwise-vacant beach bar, surrounded by empty tables. My father wasted no time in walking onto the patio—and seating himself at the table directly next to them.

This did not go unnoticed, and within a few minutes, George and his friend picked up their drinks and moved several tables over. My father waited all of two minutes and then followed suit, moving several tables over and once again seating himself right next to George and his pal. Twenty empty tables to choose from, and my father placed himself immediately adjacent to the world's biggest pop star not once but twice. So once again, George and his guest felt compelled to get up and move—this time to a table against a stone wall and behind a potted palm tree, effectively thwarting my dad's attempts to continue stalking them. Not that it mattered: by that point, I had arrived on the scene.

"I followed them from table to table," my dad said proudly. "But for some reason, now they're hiding behind that tree."

And there I saw them—or more accurately, saw him: George Michael, the man whose full name—Georgios Panayiotou—I had practiced saying aloud (for when we said our vows) and whose every biographical detail I had memorized (favorite color: blue. Least favorite food: okra). Less than twenty-five yards away from me. He was really sitting there, laughing with a man I assumed was an old childhood pal or something.

My mom was ready with her ever-present piece of paper and felt-tip pen. "Go ahead, honey," she said, once again urging me to go after an autograph.

I took a moment to steady myself. I was only a little older than I had been during my Robert Downey Jr. outburst, and with all due respect to Iron Man, my love for George far outweighed any fleeting crush I'd had on Robert. If ever there was a chance of melting down once again, this was it. Not to mention, this was hardly a large public gathering. Judging from how often George and his buddy were making eye contact with each other, they were clearly locked in some sort of meaningful conversation. Despite my misgivings, I knew I would never forgive myself if I didn't manage to at least say hello, and I once again realized the worst case scenario was completely survivable. If he said no, I'd be disappointed, but I'd live. I had nothing to lose. *"You're not going to cry, you're not going to cry, you're not going to cry,"* I chanted to myself as I walked toward George's table.

Given my father's antics, by that point George and his buddy didn't seem particularly irked to see me approach. Obviously, they were now resigned to the fact that they were going to be disturbed no matter where they fled.

"I'm so sorry to bother you," I said, my voice shaking but not near tears; I had learned to rein it in a bit. "But do you think I could have your autograph?"

George smiled at me kindly and put down his glass.

"Sure, not a problem," he said, but didn't extend his hand. Then he looked me in the eyes and my heart skipped a beat.

"But one question first," George said, raising one eyebrow. For one fleeting second I let myself hope that the question was, "Would you like to marry me even though it would be illegal in most states?" Then I listened to what he was actually saying.

"That man you were talking to over there," George asked, nodding his head toward an area behind me. "Who is he?"

I looked back over at my father, who was sitting with my mother and giving me a thumbs-up while grinning wildly from halfway across the restaurant.

"Uh, him?" I asked nervously, gesturing toward my dad but hoping they meant someone, anyone else. The bartender, maybe?

"Yes, him," George said. "What I mean is, do we know him or something? Is he someone who has maybe met us before? Are we supposed to know who he is?"

"Uh...no," I said uncertainly. "I mean, I really don't think so. That's just my dad. He's just...my dad."

"Oh," George said. "Well, all right then." He took the paper and signed it with his name but no message, not that it would make me cherish it any less. I thanked him profusely, wished him and his guest a good evening, and scurried back to my parents.

"What did they say to you?" my mom asked.

"He wanted to know if they're supposed to know you, *Dad*," I said, emphasizing his name like it was the most ridiculous word I'd ever had to utter.

"Hmmm..." my father pondered. "They probably thought I was Tom Courtenay."

I'm aware that absolutely no one reading this will have the first idea who Tom Courtenay is. He's a British film and stage actor who was part of the New Wave era of British films in the sixties—i.e., when George Michael was still a child— and most notably had a supporting role in *Dr. Zhivago*. He looks nominally like my father in the sense that they both have brown hair, strong noses, and human bodies. I'm going to go out on a limb and say with some certainty that George Michael and his good friend had no idea who Tom Courtenay was, and probably still do not. Nevertheless, while my father's invoking an obscure British thespian won't tell you much about how he looks, just know that it explains a lot about why I'm now the sort of person who uses words like "innumerate" and "gravitas" in a sentence. You say "pretentious"; Dad and I say "erudite."

In the week that followed, my mother essentially invented the photo bomb, floating on her raft absurdly close to a black-Speedo-clad George while my father claimed to take pictures of her, all while actually focusing instead on George. The resulting photos show a justifiably wary George front-and-center with my mother's butt floating just out of view.

When I returned to school the following week, everyone began trading their vacation stories. I was ready to launch into the incredible tale of my encounter with George, but I stopped short. I knew if I talked about it, I'd have to roll my eyes and let sarcasm coat every word. I'd have to offer details about how "lame" he was and how "gross" he looked. I didn't want to do that. I couldn't do that. I stayed silent.

Luckily, over the years, I got better at embracing my preference for bubblegum-flavored culture. Living in England was a start: nothing like the land that gave us Monty Python to give you freedom to celebrate the deeply silly. The advent of irony also helped: whether I'm being sincere or not when I discuss my love for the animated series *Jem and the Holograms* really doesn't seem to matter to my hipster friends who bought me the DVD boxed set for my birthday.

There are still moments, however, when I once again fear my tastes are too pedestrian. In the town where I now live, I belong to a book club attended by some of the most brilliant women I've ever met. They are doctors and lawyers and writers and just generally sarcastic, witty, erudite, insightful whip-smart ladies whose company I feel honored to enjoy. At every single one of our gatherings, however, toward the end, there is a moment that goes like this:

Brilliant Lawyer: So what should we read next month?

Brilliant Doctor: I'd really like something meaty. Has anyone read that book that the *New York Times* just reviewed, about the Serbian orphans battling blindness? The one set against the backdrop of the fall of the Ottoman Empire?

Brilliant Writer: Oh, that sounds good. I heard about that on NPR.

Brilliant Lawyer: And it was originally written in Serbian but I hear the translation is fantastic! And it's only five hundred pages long so it should go by quickly. I'm pretty sure it just won the Ida McCorklestein Prize for Obscure Literature. Sounds like a good option to me!

Me (muttering to myself): Soooo...I guess no one wants to talk about that new Jennifer Weiner novel about the funny, smart, slightly chubby girl who finds happiness against the odds?

It should be noted that I occasionally succeed at shoving my preference for easily digestible literature down the throats of my fellow book club members, and every single time the book has turned out to be abysmal (here's a tip: avoid the one about the promiscuous girl who learns nothing and is generally an atrocious human being from start to finish) which makes me silently vow not to proclaim my mainstream preferences ever again—until I wind up reading a novel the following month that contains graphic descriptions of worm-infested soldiers suffering from dysentery. Four weeks later, there I sit, swearing to my genius pals that I've heard nothing but amazing things about the sequel to *The Devil Wears Prada*. I will admit, of course, that these women have pushed me to greater heights: thanks to them, I read *The Goldfinch* (all 771 pages of it) and actually enjoyed it. But not as much as I enjoy being able to tell people I've read *The Goldfinch*.

Now, over two decades after I was a George-denier, I had landed at *People*, a magazine that unabashedly celebrates pop culture. The Fonz used to be on our cover. The Bachelor currently is. In one of the first story meetings I attended, someone began talking about a celebrity with a breast cancer story to share. Soon the conversation had pivoted into a discussion of other stars who had chronicled their breast cancer fights with the magazine—Sheryl Crow, Christina Applegate.

"Remember when we did that first big mastectomy story? With that blonde actress who was on that show?" one editor said while others tried to remember which star she meant.

"Ann Jillian," I said, almost reflexively.

"Right! Her!" the editor said. "It was a big deal back then. She was still on that waitress show, whatever it was called..."

"*It's a Living*," I said, finishing the sentence.

Another editor looked at me.

"Are you even old enough to have watched that show?" she asked.

"I even remember the name of the restaurant where they all worked. Above the Top. Because it was a rooftop restaurant at the top of a skyscraper," I replied. "I can probably name half the cast, too. Crystal Bernard, the actress from *Wings*, got her start on that show. So did Susan Sullivan, before she became Maggie on *Falcon Crest*."

The words had spilled out of my mouth before my brain could register how bizarrely obsessed they might have made me sound.

"Okay, you're scaring me a little bit," the editor replied. I looked down, embarrassed that I had revealed what a TV geek I truly was. Then the editor spoke again.

"That's completely awesome," she added.

The real eye-opener came a few days later, when I attended my first pitch meeting, in which the editors for each section suggested stories they thought would be good for upcoming issues.

Julie Dam, a Harvard-educated whip-smart editor who had previously worked for *Time* magazine's London bureau and had published a novel already, oversaw the music coverage for the magazine. She excitedly suggested a comeback feature to Larry.

"George Michael is touring for the first time in fifteen years," she explained. In the years since I'd left him behind that palm tree in the Virgin Islands, George had experienced a rather spectacular fall from grace. In 1998, he'd been busted propositioning an undercover police officer in a public bathroom in Beverly Hills. I had worked at the *Post* at the time and helped suggest the headline we eventually ran for the story: *Zip Me Up before You Go Go.* (That's a reference to George's big hit when he was a member of Wham! but if I have to explain that to you, then the only reason you've read this far is because you are in some way related to me.) Following that, George had a string of drug-related arrests, and largely retreated from public view, with his albums failing to gain much traction on the charts or on the radio. But in 2006, George announced his first major world tour after years of semi-seclusion, and in 2008 that tour was still going strong. George was performing all his greatest hits from Wham! and his solo career, and Gen Xers like me were going to the concerts in droves.

"I think it would be great to do a catching-up feature with him," Julie suggested.

Before I knew it, I was gasping out loud.

"Oh my god, I love him," I gasped. It was as if I'd been waiting to say it for twenty years, and now I couldn't stop.

"I got his autograph when I was on vacation as a teenager and it's one of my prized possessions and he was amazing when I saw him in concert in 1990 and *Faith* is my favorite album of all time," I said in one long sentence.

Julie smiled at me and continued her pitch; that's when I noticed that several other people in the room were murmuring in agreement with her: George was great. Julie's pitch was rock-solid.

I later learned that Larry Hackett's musical taste is far more closely aligned with the too-cool-for-school classmates I once had. I'm pretty sure he's seen Echo & the Bunnymen in concert. That afternoon, however, he turned to Julie, nodded his head and said, "That's a great idea. Go for it."

At last, I was home. I had found my people—at *People*.

After the meeting, Julie stuck her head into my office.

"Hey, I'm going to go see George in concert," she said. "Want to come, too?"

As if she even had to ask. We attended his show at Madison Square Garden the following week, and the concert was incredible—and I still remembered every word to every song. I still have the ticket stub.

George's performance was amazing, and he looked nearly as good as he had in that little black Speedo. Almost as wonderful as seeing George on stage, though, was witnessing the packed arena. Thousands of women in their thirties—women who, like me, had been in their teens during George's heyday—filled the seats. I was not alone in my love for him; far from it. There were many more people like me, even if apparently none of them had gone to my high school.

Best of all, I had found a place where I got to work with such fans every day. I think somehow, as I had struggled in a job I no longer loved, I always believed I would make it to somewhere better. All along, on some level, I was telling myself: *I've gotta have faith*.

Chapter 8

Kate Gosselin Turned Me into Her Sidekick

GROWING UP ON THE ONCE-BOHEMIAN FAR UPPER West Side of Manhattan, you get used to seeing a lot of strange things on a lot of street corners. There was the man who frequented the stretch of Broadway in front of my first apartment who simply shouted "Hallelujah!" with a lilting Caribbean patois, over and over again. One day I realized he also rode the same subway I did into midtown—where he stood on a street corner near my first job and continued declaring "Hallelujah!" all afternoon before heading back home with me to continue his proclamations. I would hear him, announcing his good news, every night as I'd drift off to sleep, "Hallelujah!" on constant repeat, with the occasional "Jesus!" thrown in every so often, just for a dash of variety.

My favorite street performers, though, were the musicians.

Particularly on subway platforms, there were always a plethora of one-man-bands: a guy who'd wear a keyboard, a harmonica, some form of percussion instrument strapped to his leg, and occasionally a guitar—all of which he could perform simultaneously. An instrument case would lay open in front of these guys, and whenever my meager early-journalist's income would allow, I was so impressed by their sheer dexterity I would drop in a dollar. (The "Hallelujah!" guy never got so lucky.)

At *Good Housekeeping* I had been just like one of those one-man-bands: thinking up ideas, negotiating access to celebrities, doing the interview, writing the story, and doing the initial edit on my own work. By the time I settled in at *People,* I could no longer consider my career in its early stages: surely, after eleven years spent on such a wide range of tasks, I had reached some sort of midpoint. (This math would have me retiring somewhere around age 45. Let's go with it.) If I thought I had nothing left to learn, however, I was about to be quickly educated. *People*'s staff, in comparison to what I had been used to at *GH,* was massive—and massively accomplished. No one needed me to help wrangle access to A-listers; they'd been doing it successfully for decades. Editors refined the stories that would eventually make it into the magazine, and worked to generate story ideas with teams of writers from their section—in my case, television. But there were editors for music, television, film, as well as the magazine's human interest staff who oversaw the "other half" of the magazine: ordinary people doing extraordinary things, gripping real-life dramas (Baby Jessica falling down that well, for example) and any sort of true crime that would strike a chord with readers.

As for writing stories, *People* was one of the few magazines that kept a full roster of writers on staff, rather than doling out assignments to a list of "contributing editors" who were essentially glorified freelancers. There were staffers at *People* whose sole job was to write. I quickly made peace with the fact that my primary role would now be editing, and coming up with ideas for the magazine. For the first time since my days at *Page Six*—when representatives for young starlets would clamor for the chance to get their nubile young clients mentioned in the column—I also discovered that instead of constantly seeking out talent, at *People* the talent (or, more accurately, their publicists) would come to me. Still, after all my years of begging at *GH,* I felt confident that I was approaching at least semi-pro levels of expertise. Then I started working for Larry Hackett.

Particularly after my experience with Rosemary, I was able to look back and recognize what great bosses I'd had in Richard Johnson and Ellen Levine. Larry was an ideal hybrid of the two. He had Richard's confidence, aggression, and swagger, and Ellen's keen insights and willingness to take risks. Having come up the ranks as a journalist for the New York *Daily News,* Larry respected my tabloid newspaper roots, and trusted my instincts. But that didn't mean he was going to make things easy for me. As I had with Ellen, I quickly learned that I would have to advocate, sometimes fiercely, for the stories that I believed in. I also learned that sometimes— oftentimes, given the pace of a weekly magazine and the abundance of good stories being pitched by a slew of fantastic editors—I was going to lose. What I still had to learn was how to do it gracefully. I'm embarrassed to admit how often my idea suggestions that weren't met with instant or eventual approval resulted in my responding in a voice probably only audible to dolphins. Particularly relentless about one story I thought the magazine should be pursuing, I brought it up again and again, long after Larry had vetoed it. "What part of *no* do you not understand?" he finally said tersely. My new boss was not averse to some tough love—and he was never fiercer than when showing me how to be better.

One of the last things I had done before leaving *Good Housekeeping* was book the November cover. Rosemary was increasingly using "still-life" covers each month, and so now it wasn't merely the October cover featuring pumpkins or the December cover featuring a gingerbread house, but also hydrangeas in August, and tulips in April. For November, something Thanksgiving-themed was planned, along with a recipe bonanza promising to make the holiday effortless (because nothing says "effortless" like five different approaches to potatoes). I still felt obliged to get a celebrity somewhere on the cover of the magazine, however, and I pushed Rosemary to consider a "split run" for the cover, in which the production plant splits off a portion of the covers for a different, alternate image. The majority of covers would feature turkey, while a few select markets would get an alternate cover, with a star smiling back at them rather than a dead bird.

In the spring of 2008, a family had taken over basic cable with their adorable antics and good-natured bickering. *Jon & Kate Plus 8* starred the Gosselins—Jon and Kate, plus their eight kids: twins *and* sextuplets. They were the definition of rubbernecking TV; you couldn't look away, even if you tried. But at that stage in the family's saga, no one had much reason to look away. Sure, Kate would berate Jon for forgetting a coupon (or breathing with his mouth open), and Jon could devolve into a monosyllabic martyr, but there appeared to be genuine affection between the couple. And the kids! Oh, those kids! The sextuplets—Aaden, Collin, Joel, Hannah, Alexis, and Leah—and the older twin girls, Mady and Cara—were irrepressible and adorable. Best of all, none of it seemed contrived or coached. It was during the dawn of the Kardashians, and the start of an era of "scripted reality" where faux-controversies were cooked up to suit a storyline. But *Jon & Kate Plus 8* was the antidote to that: It was reality TV you didn't have to feel guilty about watching. An entire episode would be devoted to a trip to the zoo, or a backyard barbecue. More and more, I heard people talking about the show and, specifically, about Kate. Kate's evident exhaustion and borderline obsessive-compulsive disorder—which she seemed all too willing to put on display—was striking a chord with worn-out mothers everywhere. Yes, she often seemed like a shrew, but with eight kids and a husband who sometimes acted like a ninth, she at least seemed to have a good reason for her less-than-lovely moments.

The ratings for the show, airing on TLC, increased week after week. The family was rapidly becoming inescapable: either a new episode or a rerun of *Jon & Kate Plus 8* seemed to be airing at all hours. The Gosselins announced they had a new book about their family adventures coming out in November, and I told Rosemary I thought we should feature them on the cover that month. Given that a pecan pie or bowl of stuffing or glazed drumstick was set to run on the cover in most of the country, Rosemary wasn't all that worried about letting a small portion of the covers feature a reality-TV family from basic cable. I reached out to the head of publicity at TLC, Laurie Goldberg, and offered the split-run cover; she was thrilled to take it to the family, who promptly accepted.

Two months later, before the photo shoot at the Gosselin's home in Wyomissing, Pennsylvania, and before the interview with the family, I left *Good Housekeeping*.

When I arrived at *People*, one of the first publicists I heard from was Laurie. She was sorry I wouldn't be overseeing the Gosselin story at *Good Housekeeping*, but she actually had a different Gosselin story to pitch for *People*. The Gosselins were going to head to Hawaii, where Jon traced some of his ancestry, for their ninth wedding anniversary. While there, they planned to renew their vows. Was I interested in having the exclusive for *People*? I knew my answer: of course I was. But it wasn't up to me.

A few days later, the editors gathered for the weekly pitch meeting. When I brought up the Gosselins, I had hoped there would be some glimmer of recognition from Larry. Knowing as I do now that he is an alt-rock listening, fly-fishing, *Mad Men* enthusiast, I can see how completely misguided that hope was. Other people—women, especially—around the table nodded their heads when I mentioned how popular the show was; a few agreed when I said Kate in particular made for a riveting subject.

"I promise you, people are obsessed with this family," I told Larry, careful not to push to the point of obnoxiousness, but knowing that I wouldn't give up without a fight. Larry responded with the closest thing I was going to get to an enthusiastic thumbs-up: a shrug and a "sure, ok." A writer for *People* based in Colorado went to Maui and covered the family for the three days of vow-renewal festivities, and the resulting story was truly gorgeous.

"Maybe they'll renew their vows again next year for their tenth anniversary and we can cover that," I said to Laurie afterward.

———————

The original incident was just Jon leaving a bar, late at night, with a girl by his side. I was home, sick with strep throat, when I heard about it. In a feverish haze, I spoke to Laurie, who said she would put Jon on the phone with one of my writers, and he would explain that he was simply letting off steam in a local dive and didn't realize how it would look. It wasn't as though the paparazzi were a regular presence in Wyomissing. Our writer got on the phone with Jon, a one-page story ran in the magazine that week, and I fell into a NyQuil-fueled coma for the next four days.

Credit needs to be given where it's due, and it was *Us Weekly,* our most direct competitor, that truly did it first. Several weeks later, their cover hit stands: Jon had once again been caught leaving a bar with a girl (this time in a brand-new sports car he had just leased) and now *Us* had bought the photos of it. "CAUGHT WITH OTHER WOMAN" their coverline blared, while the story inside detailed his "naughty night" with someone who would later be identified as a twenty-two-year-old woman. The main image *Us* used for their cover was of Jon and Kate, in Hawaii, at their vow renewal—*People*'s photo shoot had become available for anyone else to use once our embargo on the photos was up. To me, it felt almost like a direct blow.

One week later, *Us* was preparing their second Gosselin cover—"AFFAIR WITH TEACHER" it would declare—in what would ultimately be a string of eleven covers in a row devoted to the Gosselins—and Larry called me with the news: The sales numbers for the first *Us* cover were in, and they were spectacular. At that point in time, *People* would regularly sell around 1.2 million copies a week. *Us* generally sold about half as well as we did, but their Kate cover had broken the one million mark, bringing their sales figures uncomfortably close to ours for the week.

"Can you get Kate?" Larry asked. It wasn't really a request, I knew. My mission now was clear: we needed Kate Gosselin in *People,* and we needed her immediately.

I called Laurie, who was quickly proving herself to be not just a publicist but also a crisis manager extraordinaire. She would have been well within her rights, by that point, to yell at every person calling her begging for a quote or comment, or worse, informing her of a new sordid twist in the tale. This was not in any way what she'd signed up for, yet she was handling it masterfully. I caught her on her cellphone and got right to the point.

"Kate should talk to us, Laurie," I said, trying not to sound desperate. "We'll tell her story fairly."

"I just don't know if I'd really trust anyone not to twist it all around into something even more scandalous at this point," Laurie said. "People just want this to blow up more and more, and I'm still hoping they might be able to fix things."

"You can trust us," I assured her and went on to explain the great care we would take in telling Kate's side of things.

Laurie mulled it over for a moment, then began asking about logistics. This was an incredibly promising sign. Details about when and where to do an interview aren't discussed without a tacit understanding that a star has essentially said yes. Laurie asked if the same writer who had done the vow renewal story would be available to do the interview. That writer was still based in Colorado, so it wasn't feasible to get her to Pennsylvania quickly. Laurie sounded deflated.

"I don't want someone new doing this," she said. "Kate needs someone she feels she can trust. Frankly, so do I."

Before I could think about it too much, I blurted out a suggestion that would change the course of my career.

"How about me, Laurie? I'll do it. I'll go talk to her," I said.

There was silence on the other end of the line as I tried to figure out if I would have enough time to get down to Wyomissing, and how we would set up a photo shoot in time for the magazine's close. It was Thursday. The magazine's deadline day was Monday.

"Okay. I think that might work," Laurie said, finally. Then she said something even better. "Kate's actually already in New York. She's with me. At the Essex House."

The Essex House hotel was about six blocks away from *People*'s offices. The next morning, I was in a suite, sitting across from Kate.

By that point, I had grown fairly comfortable with the idea of having to gently coax information out of an interview subject. Stars are notoriously good at using a lot of words to say very little, and at pivoting away from subjects they'd rather not discuss with a dexterity politicians would envy. There's the old "use the second-person-singular" construct in which a celebrity will answer questions with vague generalizations: "You never know how you'll feel about going through something like that until it happens to you, and then you wind up feeling amazed at how strong you are," stars will say about anything from childbirth to divorce to giving up carbs.

Then there's the "answering a question with a question" approach—essentially attempting to turn the tables on the interviewer: "It's interesting that so many people want to know about that part of my life because I feel like it's really no one's business but my own, so I guess what I wonder is why does anyone feel entitled to know? Why do you get to ask me about all this, or why don't I get to have something that is still just mine?" the star will query, ostensibly hoping to provoke a sense of shame in the person wielding the tape recorder.

As I sat across from Kate, who was clutching a Kleenex that she had begun to twist into a fraying mess in her lap, I started to gingerly approach the topic of her imploding marriage with the same tactics I would use on any star with reason to be wary of me. Then Kate began to talk and I realized that she wasn't, in fact, a star.

She was a reality star.

Kate had no film to promote, and plugging her TV show was the furthest thing from her mind. She was in the middle of a crisis that was completely unscripted, and wouldn't be over as soon as she was done with a press tour or a round of interviews. This wasn't a role. This was her life, and I was bearing witness to it. While Tom Cruise, Jennifer Lopez, and my dear Mariska are of course real people, they had never—and would never—give me the sort of insight into their emotions that Kate was now granting me. Offering up her life for the consumption of others—not acting or singing or directing—was Kate's medium after all, and it was what she knew how to do best. On that day, in that hotel room, she kept on doing it.

During the interview, Kate broke down in tears more often than I'd ever experienced from an interview subject. Not fake, forced tears, either. They were nose-running, eyelids-swelling, hiccup-inducing ones. Even more surprising was her candor: Kate didn't pivot. She didn't evade. Jon had said that he hadn't actually cheated on Kate—that all the evidence to the contrary, from a receipt for a purse he'd bought the young woman, to the photos of him with her—wasn't actually proof of anything illicit. I read Jon's latest declaration that he'd done nothing wrong aloud to Kate. Then I asked her if she believed him. Her eyes widened, and I prepared myself for her to dodge the question.

"I think no matter what, I'll never really know the truth. He's not going to tell me the truth. I know that we're not on the same page anymore. We're not even in the same book in the same library," she said. "He's been really unhappy for a really long time."

It was clear her marriage was essentially over, and that she was devastated. Still, despite the fact that Jon had been caught in the act, many critics continued to point a finger at Kate, pointing out that her shrew-like ways had likely compelled Jon to act out.

"Oh, it's still all my fault," Kate said angrily through her tears at one point. "I drove him to this, right? That's what they'll say. No matter what it's my fault."

Having been raised by a working mother, who loved her

career, I felt tremendous empathy for Kate. To hear her tell it, Jon was never going to be happy with her level of success—and yet he was unprepared and unwilling to match it himself. Instead, he was virtually another child for her to deal with: sullen and complaining and deeply resentful. Most of all, he was someone who had brought out the worst in her. That was the part of Kate that probably resonated the most with me.

By the end of my time at Oxford, I had been in a long-term relationship with a sarcastic and brilliant young man, to this day still referred to by my friends as The Brit, who moved from his native England to New York after graduation to be with me. But as we attempted to start our adult lives together, it became apparent that we were developing two very different ideas of what it meant to be a grown-up. His involved sleeping very late on weekends and reading all of the Harry Potter books, while mine involved obsessing over how to land an ever-higher-paying job. Before long, I had become someone I barely knew and would have hated if I had: a nagging, berating fishwife who yelled over socks left on the floor and piles of newspapers. I was a bitch who berated him for his lack of ambition, harangued him for his comfort with debt, and pushed him into applying to business school. Which he did. Which is where he met the woman he ultimately left me for and married.

The Brit and I had wound up on different pages of different books in different libraries, to be sure. That experience had taught me that how someone acts while in the wrong relationship is not necessarily a true reflection of who someone is. (I would like the record to show that I do not berate my husband. Well, not on a regular basis. Well, not about trivial matters. Whatever, he can tell his side of things when he writes a book.) Kate had all her worst moments—a meltdown while trying to Christmas shop, potty-training three kids at once—captured on tape and broadcast to the world. She signed up for it, yes. But it still didn't make those 22-minute-episodes a reflection of her as a whole. I'd like to think that I wound up seeing a fuller version than that.

I also felt a growing sense of frustration with the way her story was being covered. After only three covers that could be called even remotely sympathetic to Kate—ones blasting Jon for cheating—*Us* and other magazines quickly returned to a narrative in which she was the shrew, and placed the blame on her. "FROM MOM TO MONSTER" blared yet another cover from *Us*.

Our cover featuring the interview with Kate in that hotel room—with the coverline "We Might Split Up"—sold fantastically: nearly two million copies and our second-best selling issue of the year, following only Michael Jackson's death. We immediately began thinking of ways to follow up with another story. In the end, that didn't prove difficult. There was the official divorce cover, timed to the announcement on TLC that the marriage was over and the show would be going on hiatus while Kate and the kids regrouped. I went to her home—by now a much larger one in Wyomissing, where the family had moved while Jon and Kate were still together and at the peak of their TV fame—and was greeted by all eight of her children. Which brings me to one of the most important things people really don't know about Kate: the first thing about her kids.

Make no mistake: people love the Gosselin children after years of watching their antics on TV. But again, 22 minutes does not show the entirety of someone's personality. I have heard, repeatedly, and sometimes by experts that I myself have been interviewing, that the Gosselin children are doomed. That growing up with cameras fixed on them, and with a marriage crumbling around them, and with a parent as controlling as Kate, would lead to inevitable juvenile delinquency.

As someone who has spent several afternoons, under several different circumstances, over several years with them, I can honestly say the Gosselin children are some of the most well-mannered, intelligent, inquisitive, humorous, boisterous, adorable, and good-natured children I have ever met. They are outgoing and gregarious, and far from perfect: they bicker with each other, and can be sarcastic and eye-rolling (yes, especially Cara and Mady, the twin girls who are now in their teens). There is whining, of course. But there is also a lot of laughter and affection. You cannot leave the Gosselin house without at least one small child hugging you. You cannot meet the Gosselin children, in person, and conclude that they are destined for lives of despair.

I feel confident saying that because I saw them on what was arguably one of the toughest days of their lives: the morning after they learned of their parents' divorce. Kate and Jon, by that point fully living apart, had broken the news to them the night before; I arrived the next day.

Kate was clearly a wreck; her eyes were bleary and she looked hollow and numb. But before beginning the interview, she was adamant about keeping the kids occupied with a project they wanted to make: homemade Father's Day cards for Jon. "Can you help me draw a heart?" one of the kids asked me, and I obliged, my own heart breaking a little bit for them. Once they were all settled with construction paper and markers, Kate and I went into the next room, and within minutes she was battling to maintain her composure. Her ring was still on.

"I don't know if I can take it off anytime soon. I think it would be weird for the kids and weird for me, too," she said.

She went on to talk about how they had broken the news to the kids, and how Jon had been the one to tell her he wanted the marriage to officially be over. "He said: This is happening, you need to call a lawyer," she said with a shrug, twisting the band on her finger.

Kate told me about how sad she was that her kids would always have this year of their lives as a milestone: *this is how old I was when my parents got divorced.* It was a feeling I understood intimately. My parents divorced when I was 18, which is a strange scenario. On the one hand, I was grateful to have had a childhood that wasn't divided between two houses and two sets of parents and stepparents. On the other, I was old enough to feel as though eighteen years of Christmases, of birthdays, of memories, were suddenly invalidated somehow. Everything I'd known for my entire childhood felt null and void. An unexpected benefit, however, was that the subsequent time I spent with my father, alone, was probably far better, and more focused, than most of what had occurred during my childhood. I told Kate that maybe this would be her silver lining: her kids would now have a better relationship with Jon than ever before. "I really hope so," she said, sniffling.

As for Jon: on a separate day, I wound up interviewing him,

too. He attended the meeting, held in a conference room, with a phalanx of attorneys and crisis management experts, who had been coaching him intensely. He was very proud of himself for having avoided the paparazzi for the entire journey into New York City. Whereas Kate had spoken emotionally and passionately about her marriage, Jon had a different strategy. Absolutely every single question of a personal nature was answered the same way: "That is a private matter, and we're handling it privately," he'd reply in a monotone while blinking slowly at me. (He later quickly abandoned that tactic and sold "exclusive" stories bashing Kate, discussing their kids, and praising his latest girlfriend as the love of his life to numerous tabloids and entertainment shows.)

But after the divorce story, and after the Jon story, there was a lull in the narrative: no new developments. Kate remained the villain, though, in whatever story did manage to make it back on to a tabloid cover. She was photographed taking the kids to and from school and zoom lenses focused on the kids' faces for any sign of distress, for which Kate would then be named as the cause. She was the monster, the wife from hell. I, meanwhile, was turning into my own kind of monster.

It wasn't lost on me that I had been the primary champion for Kate Gosselin in the magazine, and I was then given a lot of praise—and credit—for the considerable success of the subsequent Kate covers we did. Slowly, I found I had gained a certain amount of swagger: I stopped feeling like the new kid on the block and started believing I was a big man on campus. During pitch meetings, I was less dolphin-octave pleading and more declaratively demanding. Clearly, I knew what was best, I thought, oozing arrogance. I was certain, for example, that the reunion of the cast of *Saved by the Bell* that I had painstakingly arranged would be a fantastic cover. Everyone I knew had grown up watching and loving the show; the nostalgia factor alone would guarantee a good sale. I was sure of it. I may have even said something to the degree of "I'd bet my paycheck on it." Forget swaggering: I was rapidly approaching insufferable.

The *Saved by the Bell* cover tanked. It failed to reach our newsstand sales target. I was humiliated, but thanks to my new boss, I was about to become something far more important: humbled.

I went to Larry's office feeling as though I needed to apologize for pushing so hard for *Saved by the Bell,* and for having essentially talked over or cut off several staffers who had tried to point out that the reunion angle alone probably wasn't a strong enough reason to entice buyers. Once you saw the actors all together on a cover, my colleagues had pointed out, the story was pretty much told: no need to shell out $3.99. I had completely dismissed that objection.

Larry welcomed me back to his couch and regarded me with a curious half-smirk. I began to stammer my apologies, and he cut me off.

"Hey, listen," he said. "At the end of the day, I'm the one who made the decision. Don't beat yourself up."

I shrugged and started to try to make myself feel—and look—better by pointing out all the other times my hunches had been right: in addition to Kate Gosselin, I had pushed for us to cover the Duggar family and the Bachelor franchise, all of which had produced solid sales.

"Here's the thing, though, Kate," Larry began, looking me

straight in the eye. "You don't always have to back a winner. But more importantly: when you *do* have a hit? You should wear your success a little more lightly."

I'm not sure why that particular phrasing, or the way he said it, resonated with me, but it struck a chord more deeply than any career advice I'd received before or since. *Wear your success a little more lightly.* Not "Don't be so proud of yourself." Not "Don't take credit for what you've done." Instead "It's okay to be happy about your achievements, just don't be a jerk about it." The following week, I went into the pitch meetings remembering Larry's advice, and did my best to neither plead nor demand. Later, when reality star Bethenny Frankel, whose rags-to-riches saga I had advocated for as a cover story, was a solid 1.3 million sale, I mentally chanted Larry's words as a mantra.

I can't honestly say I never again got a swelled head, or that I never again delivered an overly impassioned pitch that probably sounded more like a hostage negotiation. ("Give me what I want or this whole conference room will suffer!") Whenever possible, though, I did my best to let any victories rest on my shoulders like a feather. Luckily, Kate Gosselin continued to provide me with opportunities to keep my ego in check, as her life provided story after story that was newsstand gold.

Celebrity scandals tend to have three distinct stages: Impact, when the news first hits that someone is breaking up, being unfaithful, or doing something else nefarious or noteworthy. Next is Aftermath, when the other people involved— the wronged spouse, devastated children—are still reeling. And then finally, there's Progress, when the person once at the center of the scandal shows that he or she is ready to move forward and start a new chapter.

A few months after the divorce announcement (Aftermath), Kate was ready to talk again. It was time for the Progress story. TLC was soon to start airing new episodes, now called just *Kate Plus 8*. In the past, my interviews with Kate had taken place in hotel suites or in her home. This time, Laurie suggested I spend a typical day in the life of Kate—running errands with her, grabbing a bite to eat, picking up the kids. This meant getting to Kate's house at the barely-dawn hour of 5:30 a.m., so that we could ride together to her first appointment of the day: a quick haircut with Diane, the same woman who had been cutting it for years in a tiny two-chair salon in the middle of nowhere.

At that point Kate still had her signature, and infamous, hairstyle, which was known by many as a "reverse mullet." Incredibly short on the sides and in back, her hair exploded into a waterfall of thick blonde locks on top, cascading over one eye while spiking on the other side. It was a style that launched a thousand Halloween wigs that year, and Kate, at that point, was still passionately attached to it. I met Kate in the driveway of her house and climbed into her SUV as we headed out onto the winding Pennsylvania country roads, the sun only just beginning to rise. Along the way, we cut through tiny towns that appeared to be nothing more than deep valleys with a few small houses dotted throughout. At one point, as we descended yet another valley, Kate, talking a mile a minute about her life since the divorce news broke, gestured out my window.

"That's where I grew up," she said simply. I looked out the window and saw a small white house, with a few others nearby, and then we were past it, a whir of pine trees blocking it from view.

Kate notably has virtually no contact with her family, a fact which her critics love to point out. They were not a part of *Jon & Kate Plus 8*, and certainly her eight kids didn't have any grandparents from Kate's side in their lives. Kate's brother Kevin, and his wife Jodi, had once been regular fixtures on the show, but they too had turned on her, selling stories to tabloid websites about Kate's horrible temper and miserable treatment of the kids. Looking at the desolate Pennsylvania countryside that morning, it didn't seem terribly surprising to me that Kate could often give off an air of being aloof and alone. On that day, it was fair to say there was absolutely no one left in her life whom she could call a friend, and essentially no one whom she could trust. She undoubtedly brought some of that on herself. It's still not a fate I'd wish on anyone.

As we drove along, I commented on how the paparazzi didn't seem to be in evidence. Kate laughed out loud.

"Oh, they've already gotten pictures from this morning. You'll see," she said. I thought to myself that perhaps she was becoming a bit of a legend in her own mind: surely I'd have noticed a scrum of photographers parked outside her gate. I also doubted they cared much about photos of her leaving her house to run errands. I said nothing, and instead continued asking her about how she'd been adjusting. As someone who had watched the show I understood, from a fan perspective alone, how bizarre it was to have seen Jon and Kate go from affectionately squabbling couple to how Jon was now: declaring his hatred of Kate on national TV and partying in St. Tropez with his new girlfriend, all while claiming to have a product line in the works for Ed Hardy.

"I don't even know what to tell you," Kate said with a

resigned sigh. "It's like aliens have come and taken him away and replaced him with someone else. That's really how I feel about it. It's like I'm getting a divorce from a fifteen-year-old."

We pulled into the driveway of what looked like a residential house, and went inside. There, Kate's stylist, Diane, was waiting to do some maintenance work on Kate's reverse-mullet. I fought the urge to scream at Kate not to do it, to please step away from the scissors. Instead, I said nothing and spent half an hour watching Diane razor through the thick layers at the top of Kate's head and trim the rest.

Afterward, we got back in Kate's car and decided to head in search of breakfast. Kate had a particular spot in Lancaster, the nearest town of some size, in mind, but wasn't quite sure how to get there. Luckily, her car had a GPS, which quickly proved to be temperamental. Heading back on to the country roads, the GPS seemed hell-bent on making Kate avoid all highways, even though she hadn't selected that option.

"Go back. GO BACK," GPS woman said with increasing urgency as Kate headed toward a four-lane road.

"Oh, I am done listening to you," Kate said to her dashboard, before turning to me and laughing. "Isn't that the story of my life? This thing just wants me to go back, go back to where I was. Like I can just turn around and everything will be okay."

"GO BACK," GPS woman said emphatically to Kate as she made a left turn.

"I can't go back," Kate said to the car. "It's not worth it! I'm never going back! Let's live in the present, shall we?"

Things didn't improve once we arrived in Lancaster. Unsure of the exact location of the café she had in mind, Kate was unable to tell the GPS a street address and soon we were lost in a series of back alleys and side roads. She quickly turned off the device and decided to try the old-fashioned method. Pulling up alongside a seedy looking dive bar, she noticed a Budweiser beer truck being unloaded by two older men, both sporting sleeveless shirts and an impressive number of tattoos.

"Oh, let's just ask the beer dudes," Kate said. "They'll know where everything is in this town."

One of the guys had a thick silvery mustache and wore aviator sunglasses; this was the one Kate called out to as she rolled down her window.

"Excuse me! Hello! Hi! Could you help me find a restaurant I'm looking for?" she asked pleasantly.

The Beer Dude walked over and Kate told him the name of the café, which he did in fact recognize. He began to tell her which road to take to avoid a known traffic area when he stopped suddenly.

"Hey," he said, pulling down his aviators. "Ain't you that lady that's on TV?"

Kate just laughed. "Yes, that's me. Thanks so much for your help," she said. We were on our way just in time to see Beer Dude signaling his pal, probably to tell him that the "Lady from TV" had just asked him for directions.

We finally made it to the café, and Kate continued to talk about her hopes for the future, her thoughts on dating— "I wish I could find a guy like Matt Damon, but he's already taken," she said wistfully—and how her kids were holding up. She studiously avoided saying anything negative about Jon other than the alien comment. In the weeks, months, and ultimately years that followed, whenever Jon would rear his head with a new complaint or controversy or claim, Kate never responded in kind. She has steadfastly stayed on the high road, refusing to bash the father of her children, and consistently says that she wants her kids to be able to have a healthy relationship with him.

We finished our breakfast, went to get some packages from the post office, and then picked up Mady and Cara, who had been at a sleepover the night before. Summer was coming to an end, and they were hoping to go to a Taylor Swift concert and were already excited about their Halloween costumes. They teased Kate mercilessly for her choice in radio stations—"Billy Joel is good, isn't he?" Kate asked earnestly, as the twins moaned in protest from the back seat.

When we returned to the house, I carried in a package that we had picked up from the post office, as Kate had her hands full with the twins' overnight bags. Inside, I talked to the little kids for a while, then thanked Kate for her time and got ready to leave.

"I guess we managed to avoid the paparazzi today," I said.

Kate looked at me, baffled.

"You don't think they're out there? They're out there. You just can't see them," she said.

I pretended to believe her, but looking out her front door, and at her long driveway that leads to the main road past her house, there wasn't a person in sight. Clearly, the past few months had taken their toll and she was paranoid.

The next day Mary Green, one of the news directors at the magazine, came into my office.

"Hey," she said casually. "So, um, you were caught by the paparazzi yesterday."

Sure enough, Mary had printed out pages of photos from the various paparazzi agencies that contact magazines looking to make a sale. There I was: having coffee with Kate in Lancaster. There I was, leaving the little salon with her. There I was, carrying a box into her house. "EXCLUSIVE: Kate Gosselin May Have Hired a New Personal Assistant, as an Aide Is Seen Escorting Her and Her Two Eldest Children into Their Home," the caption read. That's how quickly a story can be created. In order to increase the chances of a sale, paparazzi will put the most appealing caption they can on whatever photo they've managed to take—hence, stories declaring someone is pregnant when all they've had is a big lunch, or about someone going through a vicious breakup because they were unhappy while taking a cellphone call, when that call could have been from their accountant or their vet or anyone. When I read the caption on the photos of me—one of them also speculated that perhaps I was "security" for Kate, which made me reconsider the jeans and sweater I'd worn—I was actually a little surprised that none of the agencies had tried to identify me as a potential lesbian lover. I wouldn't put that past certain paparazzi for one second. (A few readers, incidentally, went there anyway: Kate's critics pay attention to nearly everything about her, and it wasn't lost on them that I was always the person doing the interviews with her. These gentle souls would often leave comments on our online stories, speculating that Kate and I "were in bed together in more ways than one." When I mentioned it to Kate during a subsequent interview, she howled with laughter.)

Most of all: Kate had been right. The paparazzi had been there, all day, all along, even though I hadn't noticed them.

Kate was a breed of celebrity I had never encountered before. Her every move was worthy of coverage, because her very existence was the reason for her fame. As a reality star, her "real" life is fodder in a way an actor's never will be. Sure, we'll cover Blake Shelton and Miranda Lambert's divorce. In fact, since it happened, we've done two covers about it. We've done thirteen different covers of *People* about Kate and her life. Our last one sold better than the one debuting baby Prince George. Interestingly, every single time we assemble a focus group of buyers and show them a potential Kate cover, nearly every single person declares they would never buy it. Yet nearly every single cover we've done with her—whether about her divorce or her new hair or her stint on *Dancing with the Stars*—has sold incredibly well. (There were a few exceptions: no one wanted to see her in a bikini, as it turned out.)

I am not as "in bed" with Kate as her detractors might believe, and yet I will never be able to see her as the villain others have portrayed. For one thing, I've seen her cry far too many times. For another, she is a superhero simply for raising eight kids largely on her own. Most of all, I have no illusions about the fact that the success of our Kate Gosselin covers, and the access she afforded me, played a large part in moving me up the ranks at *People*. I did my first cover with her as a Senior Editor. By the time I did my last one (for now), I was Executive Editor. Working on those eleven stories gave me one more chance to be that one-man-band: wrangling, writing, and editing all at once. It also made me grow up once and for all: no longer the kid reporter or the fledgling editor, I was now playing in the big leagues.

Even better, on my better days, I'd learned how to act like I belonged there.

The Five Dumbest Things I Have Said on National Television

When a story appears in a magazine, particularly when it's about breaking celebrity news, staffers involved in the story will appear on morning news and entertainment shows to discuss it. This often means discussing a scandal or event while the story is still developing…which has led to some less-than-fantastic "insights" from me.

1. "Arnold and Maria have simply been growing apart and living separate lives over the past few years. There's no scandal, no smoking gun here."—On *The Early Show* on CBS the morning after Arnold Schwarzenegger and Maria Shriver announced their separation

2. "The thing is, Kate and Jon are sharing the challenge of raising eight kids together. They have to remain committed to each other, and they know they need each other's support. He's not going anywhere."—On *Entertainment Tonight* shortly after Jon and Kate Gosselin renewed their vows in Hawaii

3. "The Duggars have never claimed to be perfect. But they do live their lives according to very old-fashioned principles that many find admirable and inspiring."—On *Inside Edition*, discussing the ever-increasing popularity of America's most famous mega-family

4. "I would be surprised if advertisers really start abandoning Tiger. He's hit a rough patch with his wife—it's not

as though he's done anything unforgivable."—On *The Insider* two days after the first reports of Tiger Woods having had a Thanksgiving-weekend argument with his then-wife, Elin Nordegren

5. "Donald and Marla have been through a lot together, and he's thrilled to be able to give her the fairy-tale wedding of her dreams. This is the happily-ever-after she's always wanted."—On *Entertainment Tonight* two days after Donald Trump married Marla Maples

Chapter 9

Neil Patrick Harris Thinks I'm an Idiot (But That's Okay Because a Mega-Star Rescued Me)

BY THE TIME I ENTERED MY THIRD AWARDS SEASON at *People*, I had begun to relax a little about encountering members of the A-list. Sure, I still wanted to hug Meryl Streep when I saw her at the Screen Actors Guild Awards after-party because I had loved her in *Mamma Mia!* so much, but I managed not to act on such impulses. Despite this added measure of maturity, my inner voice—*"Oh my god, there she is! You love her! She'd probably love you! And yes, you could touch her!"*— still kicked in during moments of close physical proximity, particularly during the parties that preceded a major awards show, when I would suddenly find myself face-to-face with a star I absolutely adored. I was particularly stymied if I had never interviewed that person before. Absent a past shared journalistic experience, albeit one that only I would have remembered vividly, I wound up desperately searching for a topic of conversation beyond the standard praise for a performer's work. Whatever commonality I thought I could find between a star's life and my own, I sought to exploit. You're from New York? I'm from New York! You said in an interview once that you hate cilantro—and oh my god, so do I!

Unfortunately, for Neil Patrick Harris, the common ground between us is the fact that we both have kids. And the fact that I feel, as he undoubtedly does as well, that his children are completely spectacular.

Sometimes, inspiration for a feature in the magazine, or sometimes even a cover story, can be as simple as looking at photos from events that occurred over the previous twenty-four hours. During a slow news cycle, one great image can be the impetus for an entire story. One year, a photo of a beaming Angelina Jolie exiting her trailer holding just-adopted baby daughter Zahara reminded editors of just how well the little girl, who had struggled with illness in the days following her homecoming, was now doing in her new home, with her new mom. The end result was a cover story titled "Saved by a Mother's Love." A few years later, Kate Middleton wore a green lace dress with a surprisingly plunging back. It sparked a cover story called "Wow! Sexy New Kate!"

Sometimes, a series of photos will provide a narrative all their own, which can lead to a fun inside story. In the months leading up to her wedding, Jessica Simpson and her increasingly toned thighs and calves became a recurring theme: *Let's guess how many squats Jessica has been doing!* Taylor Swift showed a habitual fondness for the sort of lace-up, cap-toe heels that were last popular during Prohibition: *Why does Taylor only wear old-timey shoes?* And there's the always-fun game of *On set or just weird?* in which it's debatable whether an oddly attired celebrity was actually in the middle of filming a scene when captured by the paparazzi... or was just heading to the store. (Helena Bonham Carter can usually stump anyone.)

Yet in 2010, my personal favorite recurring theme in paparazzi photos featured Neil Patrick Harris, his absolutely gorgeous partner, David Burtka, and their stunning twin babies, Gideon and Harper: *Let's stare at the world's cutest children while our ovaries ache!* In 2013, *People* magazine adopted a policy of not printing paparazzi photos of celebrities' children. (Sadly, that doesn't mean that these photos cease to be taken: there are still plenty of other buyers out there.) Still, back in 2010, when all the magazines, including *People*, were still running pictures of kids with their celebrity parents, these adorable children made more than one appearance in our pages. As Gideon and Harper Burtka-Harris became toddlers, their level of cuteness was breathtaking. Actually, I don't just mean the twins. The entire Burtka-Harris clan was overwhelmingly adorable as they posed in Halloween costumes and went to the beach and shopped at the farmers' market and basically did things that made them look like they lived inside a J.Crew catalog. I wanted them to adopt me, or hire me to be their nanny. Either would have been fine.

That January, a few nights before the Screen Actors Guild awards, I found myself at yet another industry party in Los Angeles, this one in a restaurant with a large outdoor area, where stars were mingling happily amongst themselves despite deafening music and a lighting scheme that appeared to consist solely of votive candles. Suddenly I spotted Neil, there with David, and knew I would be wise to stay far, far away from them. I didn't trust myself enough to refrain from blurting out something excessively gushing if given the chance. But fate, and one of the most well-connected men in Los Angeles, had other plans.

Jason Weinberg is the sort of über-manager/producer/genius that could have come directly from central casting. Bookish, bespectacled, and hip, he looks like the former high school brainiac who has come back to kick ass at the twenty-year reunion. He is the manager to dozens and dozens of stars in Hollywood, and if he isn't their manager, then he has undoubtedly worked with them anyway, either by serving as a coproducer of one of their TV shows or films or by just generally being the kind of guy who makes deals happen and gets things done. I am convinced there is not a single celebrity in Los Angeles who does not know Jason in some way. Or if they don't know him, they desperately want to know him. Forget six degrees of Kevin Bacon. Everyone in Hollywood is connected by a mere one or two degrees of Jason Weinberg.

On the night of this particular party, Jason Weinberg was a mere two feet away from me. I make no pretense about the status I have in the life of someone like Jason: every single time I see him, I reintroduce myself as though we'd never met. When you're somebody who looks at people like Sofía Vergara and Demi Moore every day, my face is not likely to leave an impression. Happily, when I do reintroduce myself, Jason, always generous, says, "What the fuck are you doing? Of course I know it's you!" and some good-natured riffing ensues. The night of this party was no exception.

"Hey, Jason, it's me, Kate Coyne . . ." I began gamely.

"Oh my god, don't be an idiot. I know who you are," Jason said, pulling me into a hug. "How are you? What are you doing?"

That's a typically Hollywood question: not "*How* are you doing?" but rather, "*What* are you doing?" It's not intended in the literal sense—you'd have to be a colossal wiseass to answer "I'm standing here talking to you at this party"—but rather to provoke an answer about your latest project, film, or deal. But since I had neither films nor deals to discuss, I took the wiseass route.

"Right now? I'm trying not to gawk at Neil Patrick Harris and his gorgeous man," I said with a shrug.

"Oh, NPH is here? Fantastic! Let's go say hello!" Jason said, and before I could stop him, he was making a beeline for Neil and David, pulling me along in his wake. I frantically scanned the crowd to see if there was anyone else I knew so I could pull away from Jason and tell him I needed desperately to talk to the publicist for a third-tier actress from a canceled sitcom on the CW, but I didn't see anyone who would fit the bill.

Neil greeted Jason warmly, just as everyone in Los Angeles does.

"What are you doing?" he asked Jason, and lo, a conversation about films and deals quickly ensued. As they talked, I smiled in a way that I hoped looked normal and not deranged, and nodded along as though I knew exactly whom and what they were discussing. I was also mentally rehearsing what I would say to Neil—something flattering but not overly fawning. I would not admit to being a huge fan. I would tell him I enjoyed his work but nothing more. I would ask him intelligent questions about his upcoming projects. It would be fine. I would talk to him quickly, then extricate myself and go hit the buffet. I thought I'd spotted short ribs on somebody's plate. That would be good. After two minutes, Jason gestured to me.

"Neil, this is Kate Coyne, from *People*," he said. I offered him my totally professional smile: no teeth, eyebrows raised slightly in greeting, brief eye contact. No gushing at all. Nothing to see here.

"Nice to meet you," Neil said.

"Oh, I'm thrilled to meet you. I'm a huge fan," I said. Okay, a bit much. Still, it wasn't too terrible. Semi-gushing but not nauseating.

In the space of this ninety-second exchange, Jason had been pulled away into another conversation. David Burtka, meanwhile, was also busily talking with someone else. In a matter of minutes, Neil had become caught in a one-on-one chat with me, with a woman he'd never met before. I thought I saw a shadow of bewilderment cross his face. Hopeful to make him feel more at ease, I offered up my sole ice-breaker.

"Congratulations on your twins! I have two little ones myself," I said.

"Oh, is that right? How old?" he asked politely.

I explained my kids were older than his, and added, "And mine are both boys. Also, I just have to say...your kids are so beautiful it is staggering. I can't believe how big they're getting!"

"Oh," Neil said after a moment. "Thank you. I guess you've been seeing the paparazzi photos of them." His voice wasn't hostile, but it was clear he was making a point: he didn't love the fact that his children were being photographed almost constantly without his permission. And here I was, celebrating it.

I quickly began to feel panicked. At that point, *People* was still years away from instituting its policy against paparazzi photos of children. Eventually we would, but at that point the tide hadn't turned yet.

"So...how old are your twins now?" I said, as if I didn't know thanks to the aforementioned photos, but desperate to move the conversation along.

"Ten months," Neil said, still being completely pleasant. "It's a great age, actually, because they're just getting to a point where they're really starting to interact with each other, and play together, you know?"

"Oh, I know," I said hurriedly, relieved that the photos no longer seemed to be an issue. So relieved that I decided the best way to sustain the happy moment was by continuing to spew words all over it.

"I remember that age," I rambled. "Of course, nowadays, with my two boys being bigger, I feel like most of what I do is break up fights between them. They're just in full-on battles half the time, and I'm constantly prying them apart. Fists are flying, kicks are being thrown...I should just record my voice yelling 'No one gets to touch anyone else!' or just lock them in separate rooms or something."

Neil smiled at me and tilted his head a bit, as though what I said either amused him or baffled him, but he otherwise remained silent. I had essentially just painted a picture for him of a madhouse filled with brawling children and a screaming, shrewish mother desperate to put them under lock and key, so I can see why he might have been at a loss for words. What poor Neil didn't realize, however, is that silence is my kryptonite. Give me a prolonged, quiet moment and it will threaten to destroy me.

"But maybe you'll never have that problem," I said rapidly. "Because, you know, you have a girl and a boy, so they may have different interests and not fight over the same toys..."

Neil nodded vaguely, and as silence descended once again, I tried to ignore what looked faintly like desperation crossing his face. That desperation should have been my cue to say my goodbyes and let the man go. Instead, I did something far worse. I kept talking.

"Yes, yes, I'm sure it will be easier for you," I said, nodding eagerly, "because, you know, they may not want to do the exact same thing at the exact same moment, the way my two boys do. Like, your daughter will want to go and play with her dolls, and your son will want to go and play with his trucks..."

The minute the words were out of my mouth, I felt my stomach drop. I was talking to one of the most prominent gay celebrities in the world, who had created the epitome of a modern family with his partner, and I was busily gender-stereotyping his children. His children whom I gawked at via intrusive paparazzi photos. His children whom I apparently thought he would raise in the 1950s, where girls just played with dolls and boys just played with trucks. I replayed the words in my head and hoped that I had maybe sounded like I was being sarcastic, or intentionally ironic. My own boys didn't even play with trucks! They were currently obsessed with Scotch-taping everything onto something else in our house. What was I thinking? I silently prayed that he had grown bored enough with me not to have noticed.

No such luck.

"Or…" Neil said pointedly, with a slight smile, "*She* can play with trucks, and *he* can play with dolls."

"Yes!" I practically shouted in my enthusiasm. "Of course! Yes! Dolls for him! Trucks for her! Absolutely! Everybody can play with everything! TRUCKS FOR EVERYBODY! DOLLS FOR EVERYBODY!"

I realized I was now yelling the words "trucks" and "dolls" at Neil Patrick Harris. I needed to stop speaking immediately. Nothing I could say was going to help me pull up from what had clearly become a full-blown nosedive. Neil offered me one last smile. "Have a great evening," he said, patting me on the shoulder with what I'm sure was a touch of sympathy, and then turning away.

I fought an overwhelming urge to slap my palm against my forehead. *Well, that went spectacularly*, I thought to myself as I walked in the direction of what I hoped was a table laden with slow-cooked beef. I manically replayed the conversation in my head, willing it to seem less awful in retrospect. Instead, I only felt my embarrassment growing. I shook my head and actually said out loud, "I am such a moron."

"Oh, come on now, I'd hardly say that," I heard a jovial male voice next to me say.

I turned, prepared to see some agent or publicist I vaguely knew. Instead, I saw someone I absolutely knew, but whom I most certainly had never met.

"Uh...thank you. That is incredibly kind. But I assure you, I am a moron," I said to Tom Hanks.

As an executive producer of the HBO miniseries *The Pacific*, which was nominated for several awards that year, Tom Hanks was making the rounds of the various industry parties. Apparently, he was also busy walking around and boosting people's self-esteem.

"Well, let me be the judge," Tom said. "Who are you exactly?"

"I'm Kate Coyne from *People*," I said.

"*People*? Well then, there's no chance you're a moron," Tom said playfully. "Tell me, Kate Coyne from *People*, what is it you do there?"

"I'm the TV editor," I replied, wondering if I had slipped and fallen after my NPH encounter and was now actually hallucinating. "If a TV star does something, and we feature it in the magazine, I pretty much oversee our coverage of it," I continued, figuring any second now Tom would end his niceties and be on his way.

"Well, that is fascinating," Tom replied instead. "Tell me about that. Tell me: who is the most popular TV star that you've put in your magazine?"

It's worth stating here, for the record, that absolutely nothing about the way Tom Hanks was talking to me was flirtatious. He was more like the uncle at the family reunion who is thrilled to see you again after all these years. Now he wanted to know who was at the center of my professional universe. I wished desperately I could tell him it was a tremendous mega-star, like Jennifer Aniston or Sandra Bullock. But I knew that wasn't true. Neither of those ladies was the biggest seller of the year for *People*. An altogether different sort of lady was.

"I hate to say it, Mr. Hanks, but over the past few years the most popular TV star we've featured is...Kate Gosselin," I offered lamely. "She's been a pretty big deal for us for a while now." I wondered if Tom Hanks had even the first idea who Kate Gosselin was, and if the mere mention of a reality TV star's name had just effectively ended this conversation.

Tom's eyes widened. "I'm going to need you to explain that to me," he said.

By that point, Kate was still money in the bank for the magazine, even as our readers blanketed the office with hate mail, threatening to cancel their subscriptions if we featured her one more time. But her covers continued to sell, so we kept finding ways to return to her. I began to explain the conundrum— reader outrage vs. readers who kept buying the magazine when we put Kate on the cover—to Tom.

Before he could comment, a hand appeared on his arm.

"Well, hello stranger," a woman said. A woman who turned out to be Sally Field.

Now, before my very eyes, Tom Hanks and Sally Field, *Forrest Gump* costars, *Punchline* paramours, were being reunited. Tom let out a whoop of joy as he turned to Sally, who was there promoting her final season on *Brothers & Sisters*. But then he turned back to me.

"Don't go away. Don't go anywhere," he said. Then he placed his hand on my wrist, to ensure that I wasn't about to wander off.

Tom and Sally exchanged pleasantries and caught up for the next five minutes—all while Tom hung on to my wrist, and all while the little voice in my head predictably screamed *"You are touching Tom Hanks! No, wait, Tom Hanks is touching you! And you could start quoting* Steel Magnolias *to Sally Field right now if you wanted to!"*

Somehow, I refrained from leaning over to Sally and reciting her greatest lines. At that point, I had been in the presence of enough mingling celebrities at parties that I knew better than to think for even a nanosecond that I was welcome in their conversation. I did begin to wonder, however, if perhaps Tom had simply forgotten his hand was still on my wrist, and if I should maybe subtly free myself and head for the short ribs. Finally, though, Sally kissed Tom goodbye and he instantly turned back to me.

"Okay, Kate Coyne from *People,* so you were saying," he resumed. "Why do people want to know so much about this other Kate woman?"

I was so stunned by the fact that Tom Hanks genuinely wanted to continue talking to me that I almost couldn't regain my train of thought. Although of course, I did, and I proceeded to share every single theory I've ever had since the beginning of time about Kate Gosselin, including the one about every woman having a secret inner Kate. Finally, I forced myself to stop.

"Sooo, that's probably more than you ever needed to know about Kate Gosselin," I said, somewhat sheepishly.

"Not at all. You know your stuff, Kate Coyne. Great name, by the way," Tom said. "And after hearing you expound on this topic so masterfully, I can assure you that you are not a moron."

"Okay, if you say so," I said, as part of my brain began to fear I would succumb to one of my overwhelmed-with-emotion outbursts. This man, this mega-star, had erased The Night I Was a Fool in Front of Neil Patrick Harris, and replaced it with The Night Tom Hanks Was My Hero. Sobbing was possible, yes. But I wouldn't let that happen.

"I won't take up any more of your time," I said, my voice thick with gratitude. "But it was a pleasure talking to you."

"Kate Coyne from *People*, the pleasure was mine," Tom Hanks said as he offered me a handshake that wound up being more like him clasping my hand within both of his while I fought the urge to pull him into a hug.

Then he turned and left. Probably to go talk to Jason Weinberg.

Chapter 10

Michael Douglas Almost
Made Me Cry—Twice

THE PERKS OF BEING AN EDITOR AT *PEOPLE* ARE considerable, and some of them—standing on a red carpet during awards season, meeting celebrities you grew up worshipping, producing a magazine that is beloved by millions— are so great that to even mention them, as I just did, is tantamount to insufferable bragging.

So there's really no good way for me to bring up one of the very best parts about working at the very best magazine without inducing massive envy in others. I apologize in advance, because I'm about to tell you this: every year, *People* puts together a beautiful, exclusive photo portfolio taken during the Cannes Film Festival in the South of France. The photos showcase the biggest and brightest stars who travel down to the French Riviera to promote their latest films—Cate Blanchett, Angelina Jolie, Meryl Streep, to name just a few—and producing that portfolio requires a roughly five-night stay in Cannes. In 2013, I was one of the *People* editors sent to oversee the portfolio. Five nights, in one of the most beautiful places on earth. Yeah, I'd hate me, too.

If it makes you feel any better, I will quickly add the following. While celebrities and their entourages stay at some of the most beautiful hotels in Cannes, such as the Intercontinental Carlton and the Grand Hyatt Hôtel Martinez and others that line the Croisette—the crescent-shaped boulevard that runs along the seaside—most journalists wind up someplace altogether less glamorous. In my case, it was a budget hotel a mile uphill from the sea-level opulence and designed primarily for business travelers. Upon checking in, I realized my room featured a bed, a desk...and no chair. A microscopic balcony, accessed by a sliding glass door that seemed to have permanently leapt its tracks, had one of those standard plastic patio chairs sitting forlornly by itself, but otherwise, there was no place to sit in my room. Calling down to the front desk, I inquired about getting a chair, and the woman at reception said she would send someone. Sure enough, thirty minutes later, there was a knock at my door, and in walked a woman from housekeeping—carrying only a rag. She proceeded to walk out to the small balcony, wipe down the plastic chair, carry it into my room, and place it in front of my desk. Then she exited without saying a word.

I went down to the front desk in person and asked if perhaps there was some sort of better chair that might be placed in my room. Given my spotty recollection of high school

French, what I probably said was something that would literally translate to: "Please can I have a chair which is real and true?" Passing by several rooms being serviced by housekeeping on my way to the elevator, I had noticed armchairs next to some of the beds. Maybe I could have a chair like one of those?

"Oh no," the woman at reception informed me, mercifully in English, after looking up my room number. "Is not possible for what you are paying. For zee rate we have you in zee room, you cannot have a soft chair. I am sorry, but no soft chair for you."

This quickly became a recurring punchline between me and my *People* colleague Mary Green for the rest of the trip. Whenever something would inevitably go wrong—cabs that would zip past us as we struggled to get back uphill to the hotel, a waiter who would blatantly ignore us in favor of wealthier patrons at the table next to ours, a party's velvet rope being manned by someone who claimed not to see us on his list—one of us would turn to the other and say, "No soft chair for you." Then we'd just laugh it off. Because, let's face it: even a crappy hotel room with no soft chair in the South of France is better than pretty much any hotel room anywhere else. Especially when you're there to meet your favorite movie star in the entire world.

In 2013 the HBO film about Liberace, *Behind the Candelabra*, was premiering to much acclaim, and the film's stars, Matt Damon and Michael Douglas, had agreed to be photographed at the Hôtel du Cap-Eden-Roc (known more commonly as just the Hôtel du Cap) just outside of Cannes in the picturesque village of Antibes. This was notable for three reasons: First, shooting at the Hôtel du Cap introduced me to the world's most beautiful hotel, where I will someday celebrate my one hundredth birthday, as it will take me roughly that long to save up enough money to be able to afford a stay there. Second, it was my chance to once again cross paths with Michael Douglas since he'd nearly made me cry while warning me about the fate of my blackened soul. Third, Matt Damon is number one on a laminated list of men to whom I would most like to do unspeakable things. (Before anyone grows concerned, my husband has a similar list of fantasy names. I believe high on his list is Jennifer Garner, which could have worked out so nicely if only I had lusted after Ben Affleck instead of Matt Damon. Alas.) As far as I can tell, Matt's only real flaw was that he didn't know I existed. But Cannes was my opportunity to change all that.

Just to be present at the photo shoot—albeit one that would be roughly fifteen minutes in duration—with Matt Damon, in the flesh, was worth a nine-hour transatlantic flight. I even practiced what I would say to him: some easy, breezy joke about the location where we were shooting—I was circling around a variation of "Shame we couldn't get something with a better view," which I would say while gesturing to the Côte d'Azur stretching out behind the cliffside terrace where we'd be perched.

After two days of rain when I had first arrived in Cannes, the day of the Damon-Douglas shoot dawned crystal clear with blue skies. Mary and I arrived at the hotel an hour ahead of the shoot time, which gave us a moment to gawk at Jessica Chastain in the lobby and stroll the rose-scented pathways through the hotel's gardens. Then we set up on the patio of one of the private cabanas overlooking the property's pool and the sea beyond, and waited. Every time I heard footsteps approaching I leapt up, alert, certain it was Matt—only to find it was yet another bellman or other hotel staffer bringing ice or towels or some other unneeded item. Bored, I began checking e-mail, and soon found myself sucked into a lengthy chain of correspondence about a story developing back in New York involving a reality TV star. After several minutes, I glanced up just in time to see Matt Damon sauntering past me toward the patio.

"Eeep," I managed to say/squeak, just loudly enough for him to turn and notice me.

"Hey, how are you?" he said, moving quickly enough to make it clear he didn't really want an answer but was merely being polite.

Michael Douglas was just seconds behind him, and within a minute they were both seated on the patio. I went and stood close enough to the photographer not to be obtrusive but still to be within earshot of both men. I got ready to say something about the view, and then noticed the two of them had turned and begun talking to each other, joking and laughing. The photographer, thrilled with their natural rapport and chemistry, was delighted. "Don't stop!" he shouted, and began shooting them as they continued catching up. After a few minutes, they changed positions and stood against a railing, but continued to be in rapt conversation, joking about the lengthy press tour they had endured. Five minutes after that, a publicist for Damon appeared on the edge of the frame and tapped her watch. Time was up.

The photographer announced he'd gotten lots of great

stuff and thanked everyone for their time. Suddenly, Matt was gliding past me again with a quick nod and a smile. Then he was gone.

I sat there, stunned for a moment as I realized my biggest celebrity crush had just slipped entirely through my grasp. Within five minutes, though, I realized I wasn't exactly devastated. Even if the timing, the scenario, and my hair had been perfect, the most that could ever have occurred, in both best- and worst-case scenarios, would have been an awkward attempt at flirting, which, had it been minorly successful, would have ultimately made me question the state of his marriage or mine. In all honesty, one of the hottest things about Matt Damon is that he's a devoted spouse and father. Best to leave that image completely unmarred.

More importantly, going to Cannes is an incredible adventure, certainly, but being there was also a part of my job, and swooning was not on my agenda. The images we got of Matt and Michael were great, and that was most important. Mary was interviewing Michael later that day, and I wanted to confirm with Michael's publicist that she would be getting enough time with him and, if not, make it clear we would need follow-up time on the phone. Then I noticed that even though the shoot was done, Michael hadn't left, and was also enjoying the view of the Riviera that stretched out from the hotel's terrace.

It was only two years since Michael's battle with throat cancer had nearly killed him. During the worst of it, the radiation treatment had withered him to a shell of his former self, and there had been fears that even if he survived, he might never speak again. Instead, he had rallied with remarkable strength and determination, taking the stage at the Oscars the year before and earning a standing ovation. Now he had turned in what many were calling the performance of his career in *Behind the Candelabra* and would go on to win an Emmy and a Golden Globe, as well as lavish praise in Cannes, for it. He was chatting pleasantly with the photographer about the film when I began to debate going up to him. I thought about maybe reminding him of when we had met all those years ago, during my Page Six days, and the effect his words had had on me.

"You may not remember this, Mr. Douglas, but you told me to quit my old job before my soul turned black, and even though I almost started crying in a public place because of you, I'm really grateful you said what you did, because ultimately leaving Page Six led to my dream job, which is the one I have now," I thought about rambling on to him. But I knew there was no point. I was certain he wouldn't remember the incident, and there would be nothing gained by reminding him that I once worked at a tabloid he despised.

The truth is, there was something else that held me back, too. I realized I did very much want to talk to Michael Douglas, but in that seaside location, it was another memory entirely that suddenly came to mind.

During spring break the year I was thirteen, Caneel Bay—perhaps seeing a surge in popularity after a notable visit by George Michael—was sold out on the dates we would normally visit, and so my parents selected a different resort for our getaway, this one on the French side of St. Martin. There, I glumly sulked around in a way only a ridiculously jaded and overprivileged Manhattan teen denied her usual group of friends and her usual island resort (oh, how those very words, "usual island resort," make me want to reach back in time and slap myself repeatedly; I was the worst, I know) could dare to be. My parents, thankfully, ignored my brattiness and instead extolled the virtues of the resort where we were staying. I shot down every one of them. "The restaurant had amazing French food!" they exclaimed. The food was too gloopy and covered in sauce and the place was too fancy and I didn't want to eat there every night, I whined. The beach was so wide and beautiful! they cooed. The beach was far away from our room and the water was rough and choppy and I was afraid of all of the waves, I moaned. So to recap: I was the worst.

Then they hit upon a feature of the resort with which I could find no fault. "Michael Douglas is staying here," my mom whispered to me one night at dinner. "He's here with his wife and that's their son. I think his name is Cameron."

While I might have been too young to appreciate that Michael Douglas was already an Academy Award winner, for producing *One Flew over the Cuckoo's Nest*, and while I certainly had no understanding of who Kirk Douglas was or the Hollywood pedigree Michael therefore boasted, I was very much aware of a film called *Romancing the Stone*. I had seen it at least half a dozen times. I thought Kathleen Turner, as Joan Wilder, was the coolest woman alive (I wasn't wrong), and while I was too young to fully appreciate the swaggering type of sex appeal Michael Douglas brought to his portrayal of the film's hero, Jack T. Colton, I knew major movie star charisma when I saw it. Now it was two tables away from me, eating escargots.

So while I wasn't exactly the world's biggest Michael Douglas fan, there was still no denying that his family's presence had added a frisson of excitement to the trip and curtailed my plans to be a complete and total whiny jerk. I wasn't even sure I wanted to get anything out of the situation: a Michael Douglas autograph didn't really enthrall me much. Yet I liked knowing he was there. My dad, continuing to prove his nascent stalker abilities, reliably got us a table next to the Douglas family during breakfast and made note of the fact that they didn't have a nanny with them. This prompted my mom to swing into Bethany Beach mode. "You should go over and introduce yourself to their son," she offered. "He doesn't have anyone to play with." But with only a few days left at the resort, and the newest Sweet Valley High book in my possession, I didn't feel compelled to find a companion.

Later that afternoon, however, I found myself on the beach, bored by the antics of the Sweet Valley crew and even more tired of listening to my parents debate the merits of various other resorts. (It wasn't enough to stay at a nice place: it had to be a nicer place than any of the other nice places also on the island.) I wandered down to the surf and there was Cameron, digging in the sand. He seemed to be only a few years younger than I was. He had his father's eyes and mother's sloping aquiline nose and bowed lips. Something about seeing him all alone struck a familiar pang with me, a fellow only child, and so I wandered over to him.

"Looking for treasure?" I asked, trying to sound something between casual and cool.

He looked up and seemed to debate for a split second whether I merited a response. Then he smiled.

"Nah," he said. "I was just looking to see if I can find any cool shells or anything here. I can always find them when we go to Bermuda. But I don't know if there's anything good here."

I was an avid shell collector myself during our trips to Bethany Beach. The best place to look is well upland from the water's edge, as most of the shells wash in during the high tide. I explained this to Cameron, and we moved up the beach a bit, kicking through the drier sand. Within five minutes, though, it was clear we were going to come up empty.

"This doesn't seem like the right kind of beach for it," Cameron said. But the sand was incredibly soft and almost clay-like when wet, which gave me an idea.

"We could probably build a pretty cool castle with this sand, though," I said.

Five minutes later, we were up to our elbows in an attempt to build an epic sandcastle... which then devolved into being some sort of hill/fort when we realized neither of us really had the first idea of how to build a sandcastle.

Throughout the afternoon, Cameron was gracious and polite, never resorting to the sort of wiseass teasing or sarcastic jabs that were typical of kids, especially boys, our age. There was something effortlessly pleasant about him, as he deferred to whatever I wanted to do (a quality I consistently approve of in people I spend time with) and was quick to laugh or agree to a new game. He never bragged about or even brought up any of the considerable perks that had to be a part of his life—no reference to the fact that those stays in Bermuda actually took place in a beachfront estate so huge and lavish it would later be turned into a high-end resort, no mention of the fact that he and his family had likely flown to St. Martin on a private plane, no indication that he usually had nannies or servants or any sort of entourage generally tending to his every need. Instead, as the sun started to set, after we'd built various sand structures and explored the scrubby bushes along the beach for various creatures, he told me he was sorry to be leaving the next day.

"Well, thanks. This was really…lovely," he said after searching for the word for a minute, and the adjective stuck in my mind. It was as though he'd been taught to use it as some part of etiquette class, or else it was an Anglicanism he'd picked up from somewhere. Still, he said it effortlessly and without any affectation—"lovely"—not "cool" or "nice" or even, as might have been appropriate for someone who spent much of his life on the West Coast, "awesome." Instead, he used this quaint, old-fashioned, charming word. Leaving the beach that day, he mentioned he wouldn't be having dinner at the resort that night and so likely wouldn't see me again.

"See ya," he said with a shrug, getting up and starting to jog off down the beach. I waved and went back to our fort, and then turned to see him walking back toward me.

"Hey, listen, it was really nice to meet you," he said, holding out his hand. To this day, I can't even say with complete confidence that I'd ever told him my name. I shook his hand, and he smiled then walked away. I couldn't identify the emotion I felt from that gesture, from him simply offering me his hand—it wasn't a swoon, certainly, and it wasn't really sadness to be saying goodbye to a friend I'd only had for six hours. It wasn't until years later, as I learned what became of

Cameron, that I was able to put my finger on it. Cameron Douglas became horribly addicted to drugs, eventually landing in jail where his addiction managed to persist. When I heard the news, I could at last identify the emotion that had occurred when he came back up to me on the beach that day, still just a little boy, and held out his hand.

Heartbroken. That's how I felt as I watched Cameron Douglas behave with such poise and grace and then walk away: heartbroken that I wouldn't get to know him better. Heartbroken that he had seemed perhaps a little too grateful and relieved to have spent such an easy afternoon with someone. Heartbroken that there appeared to be an innate loneliness and sadness to him that resonated with me. Today, still, I am heartbroken that the world knows him as some sort of junkie or dealer, when for a brief moment, I had met someone so classy he made a point, at such a young age, of coming back to say goodbye properly.

Now in Antibes, faced with Michael Douglas again on a beach, I knew I wouldn't tell him about the warning he'd given me early in my career. For one thing, I stood by the work I'd done for Page Six and didn't regret my time there. More importantly, there was something else I wanted to say to him, something that felt more important. Cameron at that point was still appealing his most recent jail sentence, for possession of narcotics with intent to distribute, and hoping to have it reduced. (Instead, it was later extended when Cameron was caught, repeatedly, having smuggled narcotics into prison. He also suffered a broken leg inflicted by another inmate. He's not due for release until early 2018.) Michael had expressed relief at his son's initial incarceration, taking the blame for "being a bad father" and going on to explain that without prison intervention, Cameron was going to "be dead [from drugs] or somebody was gonna kill him. I think he has a chance to start a new life, and he knows that." But that day, as Michael sat on the Hôtel du Cap's terrace, the fresh start hadn't materialized for Cameron.

"Mr. Douglas, I'm the editor here from *People*," I said, approaching him as he smiled at me pleasantly.

"You of course couldn't know this, but years ago, as a child, I stayed in St. Martin at the same time as you and your son Cameron," I said, naming the resort and noticing that he nodded his head in recognition when I did. "I spent an afternoon playing with him when we were just kids. I wanted to tell you how much I'm really pulling for Cameron to come through this and find a different path. The day I spent with him really stuck with me."

I went on to tell Michael how much I had enjoyed my time with Cameron, all about the wonderful day we'd had together, and how the memory of his simple farewell had remained in my mind all these years later.

"I don't know how often people talk to you about Cameron, but just in case they don't, I just wanted to tell you I thought he was really a great kid," I said, adding, "I know how much you must love him."

Michael stared at me for a moment, still nodding his head slightly in agreement with what I'd said about his son. Then he cleared his throat, which either had something caught in it, or was still raspy from the cancer treatments.

"You know, I really thank you for coming over and telling me that," he said at last. "I write to Cam every week, and in my next letter, I'm going to tell him that you came over and said hello. I'm sure he'll remember that day. Really, coming here and sharing that with me ... that was so kind."

He was still seated and so he had to look up to speak to me. At that exact moment, the photographer, who had continued shooting Michael alone, snapped a few photos with me in the frame, and captured a glance passing between us in which Michael looks like the most gallant and dashing man in the world, and I am looking back at him, clearly overwhelmed with emotion. If you look closely enough, you might even be able to tell I'm just on the verge of getting choked up. It's possible I'm not the only one.

The saying is that a picture is worth a thousand words. But there's really only one needed to describe the photo of Michael Douglas talking to me about his son.

Lovely.

Chapter 11

Anderson Cooper Would Like
Me to Put Some Clothes On

JUST A FEW DECADES AGO, CELEBRITIES WERE EASY to define: they were famous for their talent. They were actors, singers, dancers, or any combination of the above. When reality TV came along, it blurred the lines between traditional celebrities and the rest of us; now you could be famous by having a ton of children, getting drunk on the Jersey Shore, or flaunting an obscene amount of wealth (or an obscenely large ass). Reality TV dug deep in mining for its stars, but even below the level of Kardashians, Hiltons, and Gosselins, there is now yet another stratum of celebrity that's been unearthed in the past five years. Today, you don't even have to appear on the big or small screen to be famous—you only have to work for someone who does.

Look at the Kardashians' social media accounts and you will see the sisters heaping praise upon the men and women who transform their hair, chisel their cheekbones, tone their tummies, and most of all, dress them to the hilt. That last person is crucial. Meet the celebrity stylist: as essential to fame these days as an agent to land you an audition, a lawyer to negotiate your contract, and a publicist to get you noticed. A celebrity's loyalty to her stylist will often weather changing houses, spouses, and therapists; her preferred "glam squad" (hair, makeup, and wardrobe) is a must-have for any photo shoot or event, even if it means flying them halfway across the globe (in first class, of course) so they can properly prep her for a forty-minute appearance.

The stylists for all three of the Jennifers (Aniston, Lawrence, and Lopez) wield their own brand of power as effectively as their celebrity clientele do. One even crossed over into reality TV fame: Rachel Zoe, the wraith-like, hyperbolic fashionista who created glamorous looks for the likes of Cameron Diaz, landed her own reality show on Bravo. Anyone who wonders just why these people are so powerful need only look to one place to find the answer: the red carpet.

Ever since the E! network began treating red carpet events with the same dedication that ESPN gives to *Monday Night Football*—complete with a carpet-countdown clock, pre-awards shows discussing in advance what stars might be expected to wear, 360-degree camera angles, post-awards shows discussing what stars did, in fact, wear, and then of course, the actual two or more hours devoted to broadcasting from the awards show itself—the red carpet, even more than the awards sometimes, has become the point. It's not about the nominees or the winners: it's about that one question, "Who are you wearing?" (Although recently, a social-media-fueled movement known as #askhermore has curtailed such queries, leading to Julianne Moore awkwardly whispering during the pre-show at this year's Oscars, "I'm in Chanel," as if she was unsure if she was allowed to say it aloud.) On awards night, every star—often with their stylist somewhere nearby—wants to stop and talk to either Ryan Seacrest or his cohost, Giuliana Rancic, who often commands a second, separate spot on the carpet. That's how seriously E! takes the red carpet: they hit it twice.

During the Emmys and the Screen Actors Guild Awards especially, I'm able to stand on the red carpet and catch up with publicists who are there with their celebrity clients. Mainly, my objective is to convince them to stop by the raised platform where *People* and *People.com* are filming, and ask them to please give us a few good sound bites on video, and a few fun quotes for the reporters. Celebrity publicists, meanwhile, earn every last penny they are paid when they endure a red carpet. Rather than being able to politely decline a request via e-mail or over the phone, they have to remain firm and civil in the face of hundreds of reporters and correspondents clamoring for their client's time. They literally have to pull their client off the platform if the segment begins to run too long or the questioning gets too personal. In the midst of all the hand-holding and babysitting the client, the publicists also have to maintain a general strategy, remembering which outlets are favorable and safe to talk to, and which ones tend to go more tabloid or reach too small an audience to be worthwhile. Add to this the fact that some of the shows like the Emmys, for example, often take place on a swelteringly hot late-summer day, and almost all awards shows are on a Sunday—meaning an entire weekend is generally commandeered by the event—and you'll see why many publicists I know look forward to a red carpet about as much as they would a root canal with rusty equipment.

Personally, my feelings toward awards ceremonies don't yet extend to the level of dread. I am, however, far more realistic about what a red carpet means than I was when I initially set foot upon one. In the weeks before I attended the Emmys for the first time, I made no fewer than four trips to the nearest department store and bought six different dresses. Those dresses—by designers including Donna Karan and Calvin Klein—each cost more than all the other clothes in my closet combined. I modeled each option repeatedly for my bewildered husband and brutally honest mother, the former of whom said everything looked great, and the latter of whom, I suspected, was subtly pushing me toward anything that reminded her of the smocked sailor dresses she used to make me wear when I was a child. Ultimately, I chose a black, satin-and-lace spaghetti-strapped cocktail dress that I painstakingly accessorized with just the right shoes, purse, earrings, and Spanx. I brought it to Los Angeles in a garment bag that I guarded with my life. The morning of the awards, I got my hair and makeup professionally done. My day began at 8 a.m.; I stepped onto the carpet at 3 p.m. that afternoon. A colleague spotted me and rushed over, I was sure, with a compliment. I was right.

"Oh my god," she gushed. "Have you seen how amazing Blake Lively looks? I could die over her dress."

I looked around. Some of the most beautiful stars in the world surrounded me, and they were at the very top of their game: entire battalions of stylists, makeup artists, and hair gurus—not to mention trainers, nutritionists, and professional spray-tanners—had made sure of it. The way I looked was absolutely irrelevant. You can put a tiara on the world's most adorable pig and she still isn't going to blend in with the thoroughbreds galloping past.

Then I noticed what another one of my colleagues was wearing: a flattering black suit. Kitten heels that were about two inches in height. A tasteful, sparkling necklace. Just looking at her made my feet—in their ridiculous four-inch heels—ache and the waistband of my Spanx dig in a little tighter. By the end of the night, my feet were swollen, and my stomach was a mess—both from the Spanx and the fact that no food is served during the telecast, so I hadn't eaten for nearly nine hours.

These days, while I certainly don't wear sweatpants on the red carpet, I've dialed back my efforts. I now have a rotation of roughly six, decidedly noncouture dresses (Banana Republic and J.Crew are my best friends) that I choose from, along with a note on my iPhone keeping track of what I wore when, so that I don't repeat the SAG 2014 dress at the Oscars just a few months later. It took only that one evening attending several awards-show after-parties to teach me that four-inch heels and I do not now and never will get along. I returned home and found the website for Easy Spirit (you may recall the iconic "Looks like a pump, feels like a sneaker" jingle) and bought several sensible pairs of two-and-a-half-inch-high heels. Lastly, I learned to stuff my purse with as much candy as possible from the backseat goody basket of the limo that *People* supplies to take us staffers to the event. If I can make it off the carpet without polishing off my peanut M&M's, I consider the night a success.

I've come to accept that when it comes to celebrity style, there is no point in trying to compete in the big leagues. I'm likely never going to wear a gown that cost more than my first car (even though my first car was a used nineteen-year-old MINI Cooper with basically no brakes). Furthermore, working at *People* doesn't require the same wardrobe as working at, say, *Vogue*: stiletto heels and pencil skirts aren't exactly the uniform of most of the staff (though all bets are off when it comes to our fashion writers and editors—of course they always look impeccable). At a weekly magazine like *People,* every Monday night means most of the staff is at work well after 10 p.m. finalizing that week's issue. An outfit that requires Spanx is neither ideal nor necessary when you're eating your second slice of cold pizza while watching *The Bachelor* on your office TV set and waiting for a fact-checker to tell you if your story on Kim Kardashian's new mansion is ready for printing. These days, I'm happy if I dress myself in something that is comfortable, flattering, and not falling apart. Those would seem to be three fairly easy requirements to fulfill, and it's generally not a big deal if what I'm wearing isn't exactly haute couture. Unless, of course, that happens to be the day that I'm asked to appear in front of millions of television viewers.

When I have the occasion to promote stories in the magazine on TV, these appearances are generally in the same half dozen places: morning shows like the *Today* show and *Good Morning America*, or evening shows like *Entertainment Tonight* and *Access Hollywood*. Generally, the morning shows are live and the evening shows are pretaped somewhere within *People*'s offices. I particularly enjoy doing live television because there's a level of excitement to it—anything can happen!—and I appreciate that whatever I say can't be edited into a tiny little sound bite that might be taken out of context. Usually, I'm discussing a celebrity who has just gotten married or given birth or broken up or died. It's rare that I'll discuss anything hugely controversial—and even rarer that I'll be doing it with a journalist looking to really grill me on the topic.

I almost never did live evening shows, as they generally focused on hard news, not entertainment. The one exception was during the height of the Kate Gosselin marriage implosion, when I appeared live via satellite on *Larry King Live*. Beforehand, the *People* publicist had warned me about Larry King's unorthodox interviewing style.

"Larry can ask questions that can seem, um, a little out of left field," she began.

I tried to think of a possible, truly odd scenario.

"Like... he'll ask me whether Jon being Asian was an issue in their marriage?" I wondered.

"Um, no," the publicist said. "More like, Is the fact that you and Kate have the same name more than a coincidence?"

I laughed and felt sure he wouldn't go quite that far off the rails. In the end I was almost right. The segment went off without a hitch and I talked quite competently about the many factors that had caused the Gosselin marriage to fail. Meanwhile, a "media expert" sitting with Larry in his Los Angeles studio weighed in on the voyeurism of watching a relationship fall apart. That particular element of the conversation, about the willingness of the American public to view nearly anything, sparked one last question from Larry.

"Kate Coyne," he barked at me via the satellite feed. "We're watching this family ripped apart, and it makes me wonder, what *won't* we watch? Isn't it only a matter of time before this all leads to...*murder*?"

I fought the urge to let my jaw drop.

"I'm sorry...meaning, Jon and Kate are going to wind up murdering each other?" I asked.

"No, not them," Larry said, sounding exasperated. "I mean, sooner or later, aren't we just going to start tuning in to watch someone murder somebody else?"

I paused and tried to think of how to possibly answer him.

"Oh, I don't know, Larry," I said at last. "I'd like to give the American public—and even American TV networks—a little more credit than that."

Larry seemed unconvinced. It was the last time I appeared on his show.

Years later, I finally got another opportunity to tackle a live evening news program. In January 2014, the Mia Farrow–Woody Allen scandal was once again making head-lines after it was announced that Woody would receive a lifetime-achievement award at the Golden Globes, prompt-ing Mia and her daughter Dylan to come forward to remind the world of their contention that Woody had molested Dylan when she was a child. Woody—with the support of one of Mia's other adopted children, Moses—vehemently denied any misconduct, as he always had. *People* had run a lengthy story about the entire mess, and now CNN was picking up the story.

I arrived at work one wintry morning to have two strange things happen. First, the publicist for the magazine wanted to know if I was interested in appearing live on *Anderson Cooper 360* that evening to talk about the controversy. The chance to appear on live evening television again was a thrill; even better was that I'd get to meet Anderson Cooper, whose charm and elegance invoked zero Larry King–induced fears. Anyone who is pals with Kathy Griffin is aces in my book. I told the publicist I would love to do the show.

The second strange thing that happened to me that day was that my bra tried to kill me.

I had followed my usual rule of three when picking an outfit that morning: comfortable, flattering, and not falling apart. But clearly, I hadn't exercised enough discretion when selecting undergarments. Walking down my office hallway, I suddenly heard a subtle *ping!* and then a stabbing pain underneath my left breast. My bra strap had broken while also sending part of the underwire, now protruding from the fabric, straight toward my rib cage. I ducked into the ladies room and removed the offending item, which now resembled something that could be used as a shank in prison. There was no saving the bra/torture device, and so I threw it in the trash.

I was wearing a thin silk blouse with a gray-and-white cardigan over it. The cardigan was chunky enough—and I am not so enormously endowed—that I decided I could get away without dashing out on my lunch break for a new bra. Who would really notice if the sweet chariots were swinging a bit lower than usual? Within an hour, I had even forgotten I was without my usual level of support, which might say something about how accustomed I am to feeling unencumbered (and which is also why it's good I rarely run into people I know on the weekends).

The rest of the day was uneventful and before long, it was time to head to the CNN offices. I was having my hair and makeup touched up while reading over the details of the story one last time when the show's producer came in to talk over the segment with me. He looked at my clothes and suddenly stopped.

"Oh," he said, looking at my sweater. "That's going to moiré."

On television, certain patterns will seem to vibrate and blur together: houndstooth plaid, herringbone, small gingham checks. The result is called a moiré effect, where the offending fabric reads on-screen as a big, eye-straining swirl.

My cardigan was a prime candidate for moiré: a highly contrasting zigzag knit, which would be a nightmare on screen. It hadn't even occurred to me, but clearly, it was going to be a problem.

"I'm wearing a blouse underneath, I can just go on with that," I said. The producer looked relieved.

"Okay great," he said, before running through the questions with me. I finished up with hair and makeup, took off the cardigan, and headed onto the set, where Anderson hadn't yet taken his position behind his desk.

I didn't even remember I was braless. That is, until the chilly air of the studio hit me as I took my seat. An audio guy began pinning a small microphone just under my collar as I started to realize a serious problem was quickly developing. Let's just say my sharp journalistic mind wasn't the only thing on high alert.

"Uh ... it's pretty cold in here, huh?" I said to the audio guy.

"Yeah, I'd say so," he said, averting his eyes.

I looked down at my chest in a panic and sure enough: I looked like a far less sexy version of the famous Farrah Fawcett red bathing suit poster. Additionally, what had seemed like an opaque blouse was now, under the glare of the studio lights, appearing significantly more translucent in one key area. Two key areas, to be exact.

My mind began to race: Was there enough time to flag down a wardrobe person? Maybe tape would somehow help? Two Band-Aids, perhaps? Soon I was out of time to consider my options; Anderson walked onto the set and took a seat, smiling at me and introducing himself with an outstretched hand.

"This is really crazy, huh?" he said, which I hoped was in reference to Woody and Mia and not my anatomy.

Don't look at my breasts, don't look at my breasts, don't look at my breasts, I silently willed him.

The producer started counting down as the show returned from commercial break, and then a taped segment recapping all that had gone down between Woody and Mia began to play. I took one last glance down and confirmed that, yes, I was about to look truly indecent on live television.

Anderson faced the camera and began to speak about the story, and then he was introducing me. I did the only thing I could think of and folded my arms across my chest. That's where they stayed for the rest of the segment, making me look like I was defensively standing my ground against a potential verbal assault—or like a genie about to blink herself back into a bottle. Unlike with Larry King, I didn't have to worry that Anderson was going to do anything embarrassing. I was taking care of that all by myself.

Coco Chanel famously said, "Dress shabbily, they notice the dress. Dress impeccably, they notice the woman." To which I would add: Dress hastily, and they'll notice you desperately trying to cover up your nipples.

Like Janet Jackson before me, I had suffered a wardrobe malfunction on national television. Unlike Janet—and all the stars who glide past me on the red carpet—I do not have a stylist and never will. Because even if I am practically exposing myself to millions of viewers, I doubt it will cause a national incident. I also sincerely doubt anyone will ever ask me, "Who are you wearing?"

But the answer, incidentally, now and forever, is this: a really, really durable Maidenform bra.

Three Pieces of Celebrity-Worn
Clothing I Now Own

When a celebrity is photographed for a magazine, stylists bring racks and racks of clothing. Most of it is never worn. Some of it is worn and then returned back to the designer. Some of it is worn and winds up in my closet.

1. **Jane Fonda's Suede Pants.** We photographed Jane for an inside story in *Good Housekeeping*, and in one series of photos, she wore a beautiful pair of buttery-soft, golden-brown suede pants by Dolce & Gabbana. During the shoot, a glass of water got knocked over and soaked the hem of one of the legs, and the stylist announced they wouldn't be able to return to the designers' showroom. Once the pants dried, there was no water mark visible, but the stylist had already billed us for the pants, and the magazine had covered the cost. They were hanging in my office by that point, so I brought them home—where I was able to fit into them once, for twenty minutes, following the Great Stomach Flu of 2007. They have never made it past my thighs since. Jane Fonda is in incredible shape.

2. **Paula Deen's Sweater.** When she was shot for the cover of *Good Housekeeping*, she wore an Eileen Fisher, loose-knit tunic sweater the same aquamarine color as her eyes. We pinned and tucked it just enough that the stylist said it couldn't go back afterward, and instead it became my

very own. I wore it throughout pregnancy, which is not a comment on Paula Deen's shape at the time we photographed her and more of a comment on the wonderfully forgiving cut of Eileen Fisher clothing.

3. **Cindy Crawford's White Shirt.** For an issue of *Good Housekeeping* devoted to the bond between sisters, we photographed Cindy with her two sisters, Danielle and Chris. Danielle was a new mom who lived near the shoot location, and Danielle's husband and infant son stopped by that day. Cindy encouraged them to take a few shots with the photographer, and to have the baby be naked in the photos. To demonstrate, Cindy stepped onto the set cradling the sleepy baby boy, holding him against her chest, in the white linen shirt we had styled her in. At that very moment, her nephew decided to take a rather dramatic poop, covering Cindy. She was an incredibly good sport about it and cleaned herself up in a nearby restroom. For reasons I will never understand, the shirt was not thrown away but was instead sent off to be laundered. It came back spotless, and then wound up in my possession, even though I could not even begin to button it across my chest. Let's decide that the reason for that has everything to do with my heaving bosom and nothing to do with back fat.

Chapter 12

Most of Hollywood Thinks
I'm a Drug Addict

OVER THE PAST HALF DECADE OR SO IN HOLLY-wood, something truly fantastic has happened. Several female TV and film stars have landed at the top of the A-list...without looking like they starved themselves to get there. Mindy Kaling, Melissa McCarthy, Lena Dunham, Amy Schumer—and yes, there is probably something to be said about the fact that the aforementioned are all comedians—have accomplished so much, from winning Emmys to starring in their own shows and feature films. But I'm almost equally impressed by what they haven't done: lied, apologized, or otherwise felt the need to make any excuses for the fact that they don't look like the super-thin starlets that otherwise populate Hollywood.

Here are some of the biggest lies size 0 (and under) celebrities tell about their weight:

1. "I don't even really work out. I chase my kids around and believe me, that's enough of a workout!"
2. "I eat around two thousand calories a day. But I eat really, really clean. I find I don't really crave sugar or flour anymore. So I just stick to chicken, fish, grilled veggies. I absolutely looove kale."
3. "I just have a really fast metabolism. I don't have it in me to diet."
4. "I eat like a horse. All the time. Trust me: I know I look thin, but I just had ribs last night."

Look, I'm not saying that there aren't celebrities that don't work up a sweat keeping up with their toddlers, or that kale can't be delicious. Sure, major A-list movie star, I have no doubt you're gonna tear into a massive steak tonight (after all: no carbs in beef!). Yet the majority of people in this world, barring a metabolic miracle, will only achieve an ideal, ultra-trim, "I can shop at Gap Kids" celebrity figure one way: through a devotion to extreme portion control and a largely restrictive diet, coupled with intense exercise and the occasional trip to a spa offering a full regimen of colonics.

But Mindy, Lena, and Amy have literally laughed in the face of the Hollywood convention that a star has to be impossibly thin to be beautiful. And let me be clear: most stars in Hollywood? Including the "curvy" ones like Scarlett Johansson and Jennifer Lawrence? Are impossibly thin. They are a size 2 and under. Which is impossible in my book, anyway, unless you put one size 2 on each of my thighs, and another across my midriff, and another across my ass. And even my girls Mindy and company are, at most, a size 8 or 10. (Amy Schumer has said she weighs 160 pounds. I had thought I couldn't love her any more than I did after *Trainwreck,* and then she said that, and I started planning our lesbian wedding in Vermont.) So even the "real" looking stars are smaller than the average "real" woman who, if she is like more than 60 percent of the population, is a size 14. Yet a size 8 is considered truly plus-size in Hollywood, and so it's no wonder that so many stars eventually give in to the pressure to starve their way down into a slimmer version of themselves. I can understand that pressure, because even by being a mere bystander in the industry that perpetuates it, I found it all too easy to succumb myself.

At this stage in my life, entering my third decade post-puberty, I can safely say there is not a diet I haven't been on. There was SlimFast in my teens, when I fretted about being a weight I then thought was catastrophic. (I would drown a kitten to get back to that weight now.) There was Atkins, which I heartily embraced as I prepared to become a bride, and which led me to carb-free rages that were so bad my then-fiancé would grab me mid-rant and beg me to eat some bread. There was Jenny Craig, a lifesaver as I waddled around post-childbirth, convincing myself I could construct an entire wardrobe out of elastic-waist pants.

All diets have worked for me, to some extent or another. I've largely been spared the sort of yo-yo regaining that follows dramatic weight loss. Perhaps that's because my weight loss, usually in the realm of ten to fifteen pounds, has never really been all that dramatic. That is, until I discovered green juice.

Two years ago, I existed at a post–Jenny Craig weight that was perfectly respectable. All my clothes fit. I was not horrified at what I saw onscreen during my occasional TV appearances to promote something for the magazine. I was not, by any stretch of the imagination, heavy. I was also not what anyone would call skinny. And then I went out to LA for a three-day trip. While there, I had lunch with a publicist friend. I ordered my usual, a Cobb salad—a salad that is basically in the witness-protection program as it comes with cheese and bacon and avocado. My friend studied the menu and then turned to the waitress.

"I'll have a side order of broccoli..." she began.

And then she stopped talking.

She'd ordered a bowl of broccoli on the side of her... nothing. All she ordered was a bowl of broccoli. Even worse, the LA waitress had simply smiled and jotted it down before going on her way.

"That can't possibly be all you're having," I said to my friend, incredulous.

"Oh, there's a ton of fiber in here," she replied. "I'll be so full. Besides, I had some green juice right before I got here."

For those who are unaware, green juice is now as ubiquitous as plastic surgeons and fourth wives in Hollywood. A liquefied combo of kale, spinach, parsley, and as little added sweetness from fruit as possible (perhaps a dash of tart apple here, a squeeze of lemon there, with a dash of ginger for good measure) it is supposedly chock-full of antioxidants, vitamins, and minerals. Green juice is the answer to whatever ails you.

In the movie *My Big Fat Greek Wedding*, the heroine's father, a Greek immigrant, believes Windex is a magic elixir that, when sprayed on anything, can fix it. These days, celebrities seem to feel the same way about green juice. Sandra Bullock, Kerry Washington, and Gwyneth Paltrow (of course) are all huge devotees.

I should have been appalled by my friend's order. Part of me—the part that ate every last bite of my Cobb salad—was. The other part of me was thinking about Elizabeth Taylor.

Decades ago, Liz gave an interview in which she was questioned about her lifelong struggles with her weight. Asked if she'd ever been a weight that she'd truly been happy with, she just shrugged and then said something to the effect of, "You know what I'd like? To get to a weight where someone would say to me, 'Oh, honey, you've gone too far. You've got to stop now.' That's never happened." I understood completely what she meant, and I'd venture a guess that nearly every woman who has ever gone on a diet does as well. If you aren't someone who is naturally thin, then there truly is no such thing as *too* thin, because thin is always going to be a state you have to work for and maintain and which will likely always be just beyond your grasp. Oh, to be "too thin," I thought as I walked away from that lunch. What could possibly be wrong with that?

Six months later I found out.

Whenever I return from a trip to LA, I am full of promises made to myself to live as the beautiful people of the West Coast do. I will eat organic. I will shun gluten. I will "eat clean" and focus on "whole foods." I will be disgusted and revolted by anything packaged and processed. Usually, within about a week of my return, something—celebratory cupcakes sent to my office, a package of cookies purchased for my kids, a trip to a favorite restaurant that serves rolls baked in duck fat—derails my best intentions. But in 2012, after years of vowing to run only when chased, I took up running and learned to last for longer than one mile, and even came to love it. Following my visit with Broccoli Babe (as she is now listed in my phone) that summer, my vow to live healthier was further helped along by an unexpected source.

"Get 40% Off Our Best Juice Cleanse!" blared the e-mail waiting in my inbox when I got back to New York. It was an offer from a leading maker of, that's right, green juice. And not just green juice: multiple juices which, when consumed in a certain order as part of a three-or-more-day "cleanse" promised to "detox" and restore "alkalinity" to my body. I had no idea my body was so acidic, but apparently it was, and it was time to do something about it. For 40 percent off, suddenly green juice seemed a lot more appealing. Of course, I hadn't ever tasted it yet.

That changed three days later when the first day of my planned five-day juice cleanse arrived. In addition to three bottles of green juice, I would also be consuming a bottle of some nut-based "milk," a bottle of pineapple-mint juice, and a lemonade that also contained cayenne pepper. That was all I was to consume that day. Doing so would give my vital organs a rest from all that pesky "digesting" work I would normally ask them to do. I had committed to a five-day cleanse, because I figured if three days was good, five had to be even better. Besides, I thought, it's not even for one full week. How hard could it be? Then I took a sip of the green juice.

At this point, green juice has become so popular that you

could likely go and find some version of it at your local grocery store, no matter where you live. (Just know that the versions that contain bananas and a ton of delicious, sweet, yummy fruit are not what I'm talking about here. Kale, parsley, and spinach, with minimal fruit, is what I'm talking about here. If it tastes hugely sweet, it's not true green juice.) But just in case you can't access your very own bottle, here's how you can get a feel for the experience. Go outside. Find your lawn or, if you don't have one, go to the nearest park. Bring some scissors. Cut up some of the grass—weeds will suffice, as well—then mash it into a pulp. Add some water, and maybe some old dried leaves if you can find a few. Let it sit for about an hour, and then pour the result through a strainer. Squeeze in a little lemon. Take a sip. If you find that even remotely tasty, know that green juice tastes even worse.

I nevertheless remained determined to detox and re-alkaline my body—but those were just fringe benefits to what I was certain would be fantastic weight loss. So I choked down the green juice, and made it through the day. Luckily, the pineapple and nut milk offerings, though enjoyed only once a day, were much better. I even got used to the spicy lemonade concoction. I kept hoping that my palate would develop an appreciation for the green juice; if not, I worried I wouldn't be able to make it through all five days. But I needn't have been afraid, because after day two of the cleanse, I stepped on a scale. I had lost five pounds.

Yes, yes, yes, *I know*: it was all water weight. Tell it to my pants that I happily slipped onto my leaner, trimmer body. Just like that I was hooked. Green juice was my god, my religion. Sure, it still tasted like something that had been driven over by a John Deere mower. Yeah, I missed the sensation of chewing. No matter: I had the Emmys coming up in roughly one month, and suddenly the thought of wearing a size 4 dress on the red carpet was intoxicating enough to keep me sucking down the juice and reordering from JuiceCleanse Co. on a regular basis. I felt I had joined a special Celebrity Mindset Club: Food was for fools! This wasn't a diet—it was a way of life! Now I, too, would have an ultra-thin body and could shrug it off as though it had been easily obtained. Throw in a few visits to, yes, a "colonic irrigation specialist" and by the end of the month I had lost twelve pounds. Before long, I was skipping the higher-calorie nut milk and pineapple juices and subsisting almost entirely on green juice and nothing but green juice. I was thinner than I had been since my wedding day, and no carb-deprivation rages had occurred, unless you counted me occasionally snapping, "YOU CANNOT EAT THAT IN FRONT OF ME RIGHT NOW," to someone with actual solid food in their hands. Overall though, I looked great and so I mostly felt great. Of course, my husband might beg to differ.

"Oh god, are you still on the juice?" he'd warily say, spotting the green bottles in the fridge.

"Don't say it like that. It makes it sound like I'm on steroids," I'd reply.

"I think your mood would be more stable if you were," he'd mutter, backing out of the kitchen.

When I arrived in LA for the Emmys that year, the compliments kept coming in from publicist friends. I was, at least, honest when asked what I'd been doing. No bogus claims about chasing my kids or having a fast metabolism.

"I've barely eaten solid food for close to a month and

everything I put in my mouth tastes like Miracle-Gro," I'd say breezily. Given that I was saying this to people who live in Los Angeles, the vast majority of them nodded with approval.

For three nights, I enjoyed going to multiple events while eating virtually nothing. In the daytime, I went for long runs through the flats of Beverly Hills. Maintaining my devotion to the green juice was easier than ever in Los Angeles, where some version of it was on the room service menu at my hotel. By that point, not a week passed without some celebrity being photographed with a bottle of it.

Two nights before the Emmys, *Entertainment Weekly* had their annual party. A hot ticket as always, that year it was being held in an industrial-chic space with concrete floors and lots of glass. As with all the best parties in LA, it made no sense to arrive before 9 p.m. So I met, of all people, Broccoli Babe for a drink beforehand, and slowly sipped half a glass of white wine while we compared notes on which brand of spicy lemonade was sweetened with agave as opposed to coconut sugar. I'd like to formally complain right now that no one at the bar stepped in and slapped us upside the head.

By the time I arrived at the *EW* party, it was in full swing. In fact, so many people had turned out that an LA fire marshal had already made one tour of the place due to concerns of overcrowding. It was easy to see why everybody wanted in: nearly any celebrity nominated for an award was inside, as were some of the most popular TV stars in the world who hadn't been nominated. As I waited at the bar for my second drink of the evening, I found myself struggling to place the slightly dorky but rather handsome man standing next to me. He had a prominent nose and artfully disheveled hair, and looked vaguely like the hipster front man for some indie band I knew I should have liked but didn't. Then I heard him order his drink and the voice clinched it: it was Simon Helberg, the actor who plays the absolutely unsexy ultra-dork Howard Wolowitz on *The Big Bang Theory*. Trust me: without the garish belt buckles and dickies his character prefers, Simon is far more attractive in real life. (Either that or I've always had a soft spot for slightly nebbishy looking guys.) Within a few minutes, Kaley Cuoco, the show's main female star, arrived looking dewy and radiant and like a prom queen who reigned over the entire room.

I thought about approaching either of them, or any of the other stars present—like Eric Stonestreet from *Modern Family* or, be still my heart, Scott Foley from *Scandal*—but wanted to catch up with some of my colleagues from *People* and *EW* first. I began making small talk with several of the writers based in LA when I began to feel the oddest sensation. It was as though I had just stepped off a Tilt-A-Whirl, yet I had barely moved. Still, the room seemed to be spinning around me, and suddenly I was acutely aware of how hot and noisy the space seemed to be.

"Ummm...excuse me for a minute," I said to Peter Castro, then the deputy editor at *People*.

I walked past him and several aspiring actresses who were milling around. I noticed a banquette along the side of the wall and sat there, hoping the spinning sensation would stop. Suddenly, a rather urgent inner voice bellowed: *"PUT YOUR HEAD BETWEEN YOUR LEGS."* I don't know why I was seized by this impulse, but I knew it was the right one.

I bent down and put my head lower than my knees, and

began to feel a bit better. So much better, in fact, that it dawned on me I must have looked like a lunatic sitting in the middle of the party in a tripod-stance. *"If you're going to sit like that, go do it in the bathroom at least,"* I silently admonished myself. Still feeling wobbly, I quickly stood up, determined to make a beeline for the bathroom.

Suddenly, I found myself feeling significantly better. All dizziness was gone, and instead I just felt a peaceful sort of calm.

"Wow," I can remember thinking, "that was so weird. I was so dizzy but now I feel so much better...I'm glad I made it to this place which is...where exactly? Where am I?"

That's when I realized I was slowly regaining consciousness on the middle of the floor of the *Entertainment Weekly* party, with a crowd of concerned people standing around me and a security guard slapping me gently on both cheeks. I had never even made it to the bathroom. Instead, by getting to my feet so rapidly, I had succeeded in getting all my green juice–laced blood to rush directly out of my head. As a result, I passed out cold. Oh—and for good measure, I took a nearby tray of drinks resting on a table down with me.

Though I've never experienced it, I assume when you pass out in a New York City party or club, the first thing a security guard who is shaking you back to consciousness is going to ask you is, "Are you on any drugs? What did you take?"

Here's the first thing they ask you when you pass out in a party in Los Angeles: "Did you eat anything today? When is the last time you had something to eat?" the security guard leaning over me demanded.

It was September. I realized giving "August" as an answer

was probably not ideal. Still, horrified and desperate to get up off the floor, I weakly muttered, "I haven't really eaten much today, no."

The security guard sighed and turned to someone behind me.

"Yeah, she didn't eat anything," he said in a resigned voice. "It's one of those." Then he and a completely terrified-looking Peter Castro helped me to my feet and walked me outside. I hadn't thought I could feel more mortified, but emerging outside—where paparazzi were photographing the celebrities arriving and leaving—to find an ambulance and a pair of LA paramedics waiting for me certainly did the trick.

"Oh," I heard a disappointed paparazzo say as I boarded the back of the ambulance. "I guess that's not for Lindsay."

(No, Lindsay Lohan wasn't even at the party, which should tell you something about how accurate the paparazzi can be with their information.)

The paramedics took my vital signs and pricked my finger to test my blood sugar with some sort of contraption. While they worked, I admitted that I had been essentially eating and drinking nothing but green juice for the past several weeks. They responded by giving me yet another liquid—theirs was some insanely sugary version of Coca-Cola, and then they returned me to the curb, where Peter was still waiting.

"Ma'am, I think maybe you've taken this juice thing a little too far," the paramedic said, and I completely forgot to feel thrilled. Instead, I found myself very close to breaking down completely. I just nodded numbly, and Peter could see that I was on the brink of tears.

"You've got to remember to eat something," the paramedic was saying.

"And you've got to start laying off the crystal meth," Peter added.

I burst into the kind of laughter that saves you from sobbing. I will always love Peter for that moment.

I took a cab back to the hotel, and the next morning ordered steak and eggs for breakfast. I haven't had green juice since, and every day I skip it is a day I pledge my allegiance to the Mindy, Lena, and Amys of the celebrity universe. (I will admit to having the spicy lemonade again though. It is excellent mixed with vodka.)

Yes, celebrities have amazing lives: vast fortunes, creative jobs, impossibly beautiful homes and bodies and spouses and babies. At the end of the day, I still think I'm the lucky one. Fame is not for the faint of heart. I don't need to have a perfect size 0 figure, or even a perfect size 4 one. When I do something wildly embarrassing, I don't need to call a publicist to come and handle the crisis. I usually just need to eat some real food.

No, when it comes to stars, I don't live in their world—I merely delight in visiting the outer fringes. The day that the thrill of standing on a red carpet or meeting George Clooney or getting a thank-you note from Melissa McCarthy (who still sends handwritten ones, even after three different interviews) ever wears off is the day I should retire. Luckily, I don't see that day coming any time soon. I am older, wiser, heavier, and more humbled than I was when I asked for my first autograph. I no longer ask for autographs, in fact, or even believe that every star is the greatest person alive who would love me if only they knew me. (Though I do maintain that Amy Schumer and I could be best friends.)

But I am now, and always will be, a fan. A super-fan. The biggest one of all.

Acknowledgments

I will forever be indebted to Kristyn Keene, my very first and very best agent. I am so grateful for your persistence, patience, insight, and laugh-out-loud sense of humor. I know who you are, and you are SO the answer.

Every first-time author should be lucky enough to wind up with an editor, publisher, and all-around great guy like Mauro DiPreta. If you need any proof of my respect and adoration, know that you are the first person ever to say "I kinda hate it" about something I've written and live to tell the tale. (Also, you were right.) Thank you for all you did to make this book infinitely better.

Many thanks as well to the entire team at Hachette: Michelle Aielli and Betsy Hulsebosch for putting this book in front of as many eyeballs as possible, and the unfaltering Ashley Yancey for keeping track of countless moving parts.

The writers, editors, reporters, and artists whom I've worked with far outshine any celebrity I've ever encountered. Thank you to Peter Castro for supporting me early and often, and many thanks to the incredible *People* staff I'm still so lucky to work with each day: Lizz Leonard, Mary Green, Samantha Miller, Charlotte Triggs, Kim Hubbard, Andrea

Dunham, Cindy Sanz, Liz Sporkin, Dan Wakeford, Henry Goldblatt, and the countless other creative spirits who make me so proud to be a part of what you do.

First bosses don't get any better than Richard Johnson, and first jobs don't get much finer than working next to Jeane MacIntosh at Page Six.

I could easily fill another book with my admiration for Ellen Levine, but suffice it to say that you have been my greatest mentor, stand-in mother, and editor extraordinaire. I cannot imagine my life trajectory had you not been in it. Actually, I can, and it doesn't lead anywhere good. You also let me learn from the lovely, inimitable Evelyn Renold, for which I am eternally grateful.

Larry Hackett: You still sort of terrify me. But I suspect that will never change and is also part of why working for you was so thrilling. Thank you for giving me opportunities I hadn't even dared to dream about before I met you, and thank you for believing I was capable of rising to the occasion.

JD Heyman, your wit, wiliness, and wisdom both infuriate and inspire me, with the latter almost always winning out. I am reassured and relieved to know I can always count on you as a kindred spirit who will listen to me vent, tell me what to do (at length) and back me up when I need it most.

I refer to Jess Cagle in this book as the Greatest Kindest Man Alive, and that is in no way an exaggeration. I can honestly say I spent most of my career desperately trying to work for you, and the moment it finally happened was without a doubt one of the greatest in my professional life. Thank you so much for being an ardent supporter, thoughtful critic, and constant voice of reason.

To the professional angels who worked miracles for me in ways I could never repay—Cindi Berger, Marcy Engelman, Liz Smith, Leslie Sloane—thank you for everything, and for being all-around amazing women I will forever admire.

I moved to the suburbs hoping for a bigger closet and more storage. I never expected to also find a group of female friends that would make up for all my loner years in high school. To the Knuckleheads of Pelham: You are hands-down the best part of not only my commute but also my life as a working mom. You keep me sane, keep me laughing, and keep me from ever feeling that I am alone. A special shout-out to Heather Bushong for being the very first fan of *I'm Your Biggest Fan* and convincing me to do something about it. (Montana is next, I promise.) And thank you to Alexandra Russello for listening to my lengthy chutes-and-ladders monologues about this book, along with so much else, as we logged mile after mile.

To age-old friends Catherine Mouttet, Brooke Gomez, Stacia Libby, April Taylor-Stackle, Carolyn Hinsey, Stephanie Sloane, Scott Anderson, Will Treves, and Virginia Eyre: Thank you for knowing me then, and still choosing to know me now. And to Jena Starkes: Thank you for always being up for an adventure, especially ones involving pigs in tiaras.

My best friend, Stephanie Eiseman, has a huge heart and encouraging spirit that makes me believe I can do anything— including move heavy pieces of furniture and eat Entenmann's without gaining weight. You are my very best partner in crime, and I look forward to riding the bus to Atlantic City together in our eighties.

One of the best parts of marrying my husband was the

family that came along with the deal. Ron and Joann, thank you for being the joyous together. Dave and Meghan, thank you for your support and the gorgeous children my guys are lucky enough to call cousins.

It is impossible to think of my father without thinking of countless multi-syllabic words to describe him. Dad, you are the most intellectual, indefatigable, beguiling, bewildering, self-deprecating, self-possessed man I know, and I love you, so shut up so thar. Frances Coyne: You put up with all that, so in addition to wanting to grant you a medal, let me also extend endless gratitude.

I know many women who fear becoming their mother, but I would quite happily turn out like mine. Nancy Coyne, you are more than I could ever adequately express here, but know that you are my absolute role model, my closest confidante, my truest and greatest friend, and, of course, my own nice mommy. I love you—now and forever.

And finally, to the greatest loves of my life (no, not my iPhone): my husband and my children. This book was a life-long goal, but it is irrelevant compared with the two best things I have ever done or will ever do: being smart enough to marry you, Dear Husband, and being lucky enough to become your mom, Perfect Boys. My love for you is limitless and eternal. Now please turn down the TV and turn up the heat.